PAUL ELUARD

SELECTED POEMS

Selected and translated by
Gilbert Bowen

Introduction by Max Adereth

JOHN CALDER · LONDON
RIVERRUN PRESS · NEW YORK

This edition first published in Great Britain in 1987 by
John Calder (Publishers) Limited
and in the USA in 1987 by
Riverrun Press Inc.
Reprinted 1998

En Avril 1944: Paris respirait encore! comes from *Poèmes pour tous*, published by
Editions Messidor in 1945. *Saint-Alban* and *Le Baiser* were published in 1945 by
Éditions Seghers, Paris. *Le même jour pour tous, En plein mois d'Août* and *Gabriel Péri*
were published in *Au rendez-vous allemand* (1945); *Liberté* is an extract from *Poèsie et
Verité* (1942); both published by Les Éditions de Minuit, Paris. The rest of this
selection is taken from *Paul Eluard Oeuvres Complètes de la Bibliothèque de La Pléiade*,
Vols I and II (1968) published by Éditions Gallimard, Paris. All poems are
reproduced by permission of the aforementioned publishers.

British Library Cataloguing in Publication Data
Eluard, Paul
  Paul Eluard : selected poems.
  Rn: Eugène Grindel   I. Title   II. Bowen,
  Gilbert
  841'.912   PQ2609.L9

  ISBN 0-7145-3995-3

Library of Congress Cataloguing in Publication Data

Eluard, Paul, 1895-1952.
  Selected poems.

  English and French
  1. Eluard, Paul, 1895-1952—Translations, English.
I. Bowen, Gilbert.   II. Title
PQ2609.L75A22   1988   841'.912   87-12125
ISBN 0-7145-3995-3 (pbk.)

Typeset in 11 on 12 point in Baskerville by Maggie Spooner Typesetting, London
Printed in Canada by Webcom

CONTENTS

PAUL ELUARD (1895-1952)

Paul Eluard was born on the 14th December, 1895 in the Parisian working-class suburb of Saint-Denis. His real name was Eugène-Emile-Paul Grindel, but in 1916 he borrowed his maternal grandmother's surname and called himself Paul Eluard, a literary pen-name which he kept throughout his life. Two notable exceptions concern the Second World War period — when he often wrote under other assumed names in order to foil the German occupying authorities and the French police — and a short period in 1946-7 when, after his second wife's death, he felt temporarily inclined to obliterate the whole of his past, including his own name, and wrote under the pseudonym of Didier Desroches. He was the only son of a financial clerk and a seamstress who were comfortably off, though not actually wealthy. They loved him dearly and they instilled in him respect for honest toil and for the ideals of the secular republic, a republic free from Church control and aiming at providing all citizens with equal opportunities, especially in the field of education. After attending the local primary and secondary state schools, he suddenly suffered from an attack of haemoptysis (spitting blood because of a lung infection) and was sent to a Swiss sanatorium in Clavadel, near Davos, where he stayed from December 1912 to February 1914. Apart from restoring his health, his stay enabled him to read widely and acquaint himself with many poets who had not been on the school syllabus, chiefly Baudelaire, Rimbaud, Lautréamont, Apollinaire, Novalis and the English Romantics. He also discovered new landscapes, such as mountains and snowfields, which he had not come across in the course of his urban youth. Finally, it was in Switzerland that he met and fell in love with Elena Dmitievna Diakanova, a Russian girl nicknamed Gala, whom he married in 1917 and by whom he had a daughter, Cécile, in 1918. His early poems (1913-1918) reveal both the impact of all these influences and the original way in which he assimilated them, as can be seen from the following lines dedicated to Gala, in which the simple style and the imagery are distinctively his own:

> Un seul être
> A fait fondre la neige pure
> A fait naître des fleurs dans l'herbe
> Et le soleil est délivré
>
> A single being
> Caused the pure snow to melt
> Made flowers grow in the grass
> And the sun is set free

In December 1914 he was called up and he served in the army until the end of the war. Like many sensitive artists of his generation, he was horrified by the cruelty and apparent futility of the war, and the letters he sent his parents and friends show that he soon became a pacifist. However, unlike the great pacifist writer, Henri Barbusse, who denounced the war in his 1916 book, *Le Feu*, Eluard thought that contemptuous silence was the best way of expressing his opposition, and he wrote in 1916: 'Let us not talk of war. It is through words that it is kept alive.' Interestingly, but at the time unbeknown to him, this was also the stand that his future friends, Breton and Aragon, had decided to take, in the belief that to speak of war, 'even if it was in order to curse it, was yet another way of advertising it', as Aragon later explained. Speaking in 1936, Eluard recalled that in 1917, while he was fighting on the French side, the surrealist painter, Max Ernst, was fighting on the German side, 'barely one kilometre away' from him, and he added: 'Three years later, we became the best friends in the world, and ever since, we have been relentlessly fighting for the same cause, that of man's total emancipation.' In 1916, he published a collection of ten poems entitled *Le Devoir* (Duty), later renamed *le Devoir et l'inquiétude* (Duty and Anxiety), and in 1918, a collection of eleven poems, under the significant title of *Poèmes pour la paix* (Poems for Peace). In the latter, he praised the simple, ordinary life which the war had disrupted.

In 1919-23, Eluard threw in his lot with the Dada Movement which had been launched by Tristan Tzara in 1917. It was a trend which challenged all established values and assumptions and which preached absolute revolt. The word 'dada', which literally means hobby-horse, was not really intended to convey anything, Tzara having chosen it after opening a dictionary at random. By its very absurdity, it was an act of defiance towards 'respectable' society. Dada found warm supporters among men such as Breton, Aragon, Soupault and Eluard himself who, as a result of their war experience, had become thoroughly disillusioned with the values of their elders. In 1919, they founded a periodical which they called *Littérature*, an ironical name since the aim was to challenge establishment literature as well as all the other ideas and institutions of their society, not just aesthetic ones. In 1920, Eluard wrote *Pour vivre ici* (To Live Here on Earth), a collection of poems which show his opposition to religion and his rejection of convention, common to all Dadaists, as well as his passionate attachment to a better life. The poem which gave its title to the collection contains lines such as the following:

Je fis un feu, l'azur m'ayant abandonné,
Un feu pour être son ami,
Un feu pour m'introduire dans la nuit d'hiver,
Un feu pour vivre mieux.

I made a fire, the blue sky having abandoned me,
A fire to be its friend,
A fire to enter the winter night,
A fire to live better.

11

Thematically, stylistically, and in terms of imagery, these few lines are characteristic of the whole of Eluard's poetry, for they convey his longing for warmth (physical and metaphorical), expressed with the help of very simple everyday words, and his use of such images as fire and the sky. In 1921, a new collection of poems appeared, entitled *Les nécessités de la vie et les conséquences des rêves* (The Necessities of Life and the Consequences of Dreams).

For Eluard and most of his new friends, Dada was only a starting point, and it was not long before they eagerly sought a more positive philosophy than one which consisted in saying 'no' to everything. By 1923 that philosophy was found: it was surrealism. The word 'surrealism' had been coined by Apollinaire, but under the inspiration of André Breton, it took on a special meaning, which was the attempt to reach a higher reality (*la sur-réalité*) than that of everyday superficial appearances, the true nature of man which lies buried in the subconscious where it owes nothing to outside influences. The first Manifesto of the movement, published in 1924 by Breton, claims that surrealism has discovered 'forms of association hitherto unknown' because it has done away with artificial social pressures and has recognised the 'all-powerful character of dreams'. Hence the importance of collective hypnotic sessions, to which the surrealists frequently resorted, and of writing spontaneously. The latter form of writing was *l'écriture automatique* (automatic writing), and although it was not the only one advocated by the surrealists, it is rightly regarded as one of their most original contributions. That Eluard was a genuine supporter of surrealism and that he owes a lot to the movement is beyond doubt, but well before he broke with Breton in 1938 in order to free himself from surrealist taboos, which he found as restricting as those of traditional literature, he was already regarded as a dissident by the leader of the school, who complained that he was a 'reticent' disciple who preferred 'poetry in the traditional sense of the term' to surrealism. Actually, it was not so much 'traditional' poetry that Eluard favoured, but plain speaking, free from extravaganza. To use Wordsworth's expressions, he rejected the 'poetic diction' of surrealism and chose 'the real language of men'. However, his *life-long* debt to the movement is that it released his natural spontaneity, and, paradoxically, that it helped him to go beyond surrealism by extending the process of liberation which it had itself initiated.

In 1924, Eluard grew tired of the life he was then leading, resenting in particular the discrepancy between his poetic dreams and his humdrum everyday existence. His wife, Gala, having gone away for a while with Max Ernst, he decided that he too would leave Paris and travel round the world. Expecting that most people, especially the surrealists, would jump to the conclusion that he was seeking a form of escape, he begged his friend, Aragon, to fight with all his power against such an interpretation. In his obituary article, *Paul*, published in *Les Lettres Françaises* on the 20th November, 1952, Aragon recalled the incident and wrote:

> It was at a time when there prevailed a romantic notion about departures. He was going to leave, he knew that people would say, would interpret . . . that horrified him. He had entrusted me with this mission: to clip the wings of the idealisation of such a departure, not to allow people to make a meal of it . . . He was saying this with fury. Quite simply, he was going to travel, to travel. Beyond this, he would not look ahead.

> For two whole years, he had vanished. Against all our friends, I had to prevent ten times any reference to Rimbaud, any attempt to build all kinds of legends around Paul. Then he came back among us. (This time, he will never come back.) He had gone round all things. Confirmed that one never leaves. He had come back with images from the whole world. And not yet with the image of things to come. [Punctuation as in the original]

In one respect, Aragon's memory must have failed him, for

it was not a period of two years' absence which followed, but a mere six months. Upon his return, Eluard unostentatiously resumed his former literary activities. He published collections of poems, *Mourir de ne pas mourir* (To Die of not Dying) in 1924, *Capitale de la douleur* (Capital of Sorrow) in 1926, and *L'amour la poésie* (Love Poetry) in 1929. [Notice the absence of any link word between love and poetry in the last title.]

By 1929 the relationship with Gala had begun to grow sour, for Gala had fallen in love with the painter, Salvador Dali, whose wife she eventually became. She left Eluard in 1930. Her place was taken by Maria Benz, known as Nusch, an Alsatian woman, much younger than the poet (she was born in 1906), whom he had met in 1929. She became his second wife and they stayed together until Nusch's death in 1946. Unlike Gala, she was stable and constant in her moods, which provided her husband with a much needed feeling of security. In 1935, he wrote to his daughter that without Nusch, 'life would have been impossible', and much later, he suggested in one of his poems that the day and time of her birth were in fact those of his own coming to life:

Le 21 juin 1906 à midi
Tu m'as donné la vie

On the 21st June 1906 at noon
You brought me to life

One may note, incidentally, that the two couples, Eluard-Nusch and Dali-Gala, always remained on friendly terms.

At this stage, a few words must be said about Eluard's political involvement before the Second World War. In 1927, together with his surrealist friends, he joined the French Communist party. Although surrealism had initially shown little interest in politics and had even tended to regard them as 'bourgeois', it came round to the view that the communist revolution was an extension of the spiritual revolution it was after, and that Rimbaud's aim, 'To change life', was the same as Marx's goal, 'To change the world'. Moreover, as the young Communist party was the anti-bourgeois party *par excellence*, to join it seemed to be a logical step for the self-proclaimed opponents of all bourgeois values. The surrealists were duly accepted into the party, but their short-lived association with it was based on a misunderstanding on both sides. The French Communist party was then going through a sectarian phase and it was looking upon all 'intellectuals' with suspicion. Whilst willing to welcome some of them into its ranks, it expected that they would know their place and accept control of their whole activity, including art and literature. The surrealists, on the other hand, believed that political commitment and aesthetics belonged to entirely different provinces. They were ready 'to die for communism', as they put it, but not to write for it. As a result, their political activity lasted only a few weeks. But it was only in 1932-33 that the formal break took place, ostensibly caused by sharp disagreements over one of Aragon's subversive poems. In 1933, Eluard, Breton and most of the other surrealists, with the exception of Aragon, Sadoul and Pierre Unik, were expelled from the party.

This did not prevent Eluard from remaining a left-winger and from finding himself more than once on the same side as the Communists. For example, in 1933, he supported the Communist-inspired Peace Movement, and in 1935, he was one of the members of the Vigilance Committee of anti-fascist intellectuals, one of the many bodies that made up the broad left-wing alliance, the *Front Populaire*, launched by the French Communist party in 1934. In 1936, shortly after the Spanish civil war had broken out, he wrote a poem to praise Madrid's resistance against Franco, *Novembre 1936*, and this was published in the Communist paper, *L'Humanité*. Earlier in the same year, he gave a public lecture, *L'évidence poétique* (Poetic Evidence), which began with the statement: 'The time has come when all poets have the right and the duty to insist that they are firmly rooted in the life of other people, in the common life of all', and went on to assert that poets need not be lonely people because they are 'men among men' — a phrase later used by Sartre when he put forward the concept of *littérature engagée* (committed literature).

Eluard's greater political awareness as well as Nusch's influence resulted in his gradual moving away from surrealism. The 1932 collection of poems, *La vie immédiate* (Life Here and Now), was still 'essentially surrealist', as he himself assessed it in 1951, and so was its successor, *La rose publique* (1934) (The Public Rose). But from the mid-thirties onwards, there was a marked change: the love poetry was more direct, and an increasing number of poems reflected Eluard's concern with the threat of fascism and war. The main works of the period were *Les yeux fertiles* (1936) (Fertile Eyes), *Cours naturel* (1938) (Natural Flow), *Donner à voir* (1939) (Helping People to See) and *Chanson complète* (1939) (Complete Song).

The Second World War continued the process. Eluard contributed to the anti-Nazi Resistance movement by helping with the production, printing and distribution of countless leaflets; by leading and organising intellectual resistance in the northern (occupied) zone (Aragon did the same in the southern zone, which was nominally 'free' until the end of 1942), especially through the broadly based *Comité National des Ecrivians* (CNE), a body of non-collaborationist writers of all philosophical and political views; and above all, by writing poems about hope, France, the struggle against the occupiers, and the new meaning of love. These poems were gathered into two collections, *Poésie et vérité* (1942) (Poetry and Truth), and *Au rendez-vous allemand* (1945) (At the German Meeting Place). The former included the famous poem, *Liberté* (Liberty), which quickly became internationally known and of which numerous copies were dropped by parachute by the R.A.F. as part of its propaganda campaign. It is made up of a series of short stanzas, each one dealing with simple objects and animals, and ending with the words, *J'écris ton nom* (I Write Your

Name). The name which appears at the end is the name of Liberty, but the poem also reads like a love poem addressed to a woman, a fact which shows the inter-relation between Eluard's personal lyricism and his political commitment. In 1942, he rejoined the Communist party, and he kept up his membership until he died. In 1943, he and Aragon became great friends again. In their own individual way, the two poets had followed the same path — from surrealism, and beyond it (but not against it), to a broader vision of reality.

After the war, Eluard's international fame was at its highest. His poems were translated into many languages, and he travelled extensively, especially to Italy, Greece, Czechoslovakia, Yugoslavia and Poland, where he was received as a cultural ambassador of the new France. Between 1944 and 1946, he published no less than twelve collections of poems, of which the most famous are *Poésie ininterrompue* (Uninterrupted Poetry) (1946) and *Le dur désir de durer* (The Hard Wish to Endure) (1946). The critic Louis Parrot, writing in 1948, called the former 'a poetic summa'. It is a long poem, not a collection, which gives in a nutshell Eluard's philosophy of life, describing the meaning of his own existence and work, his search for happiness, simplicity, warmth and brotherhood. It ends with a brief assertion of his and Nusch's *raison d'être*:

> Nous deux nous ne vivons que pour être fidèles
> A la vie

> We two live only in order to be faithful
> To life

Then, suddenly, on the 28th November, 1946, Eluard received a stunning blow. While he was away in Switzerland, he heard that Nusch had died. Nothing can better convey his grief than the lines he wrote shortly afterwards:

> Vingt-huit novembre mil neuf cent quarante-six

17

Nous ne vieillirons pas ensemble
Voici le jour
En trop: le temps déborde
Mon amour si léger prend le poids d'un supplice

Twenty-eighth November nineteen forty-six
We shall not grow old together
This is one day
Too many: time overflows
My love so light now weighs like agony

He confessed later that his sense of injustice and revolt was
so great that he became bitter and cantankerous. He took it
out on his closest friends, and he, 'who had until then lived
without wickedness, became wicked', as he put it in the
1948 preface to his collection of 'political poems'. Those
who tried to help him and comfort him had to put up with
his fits of temper. He even took an almost perverse pleasure
in hurting them and in hurting himself. Then he recovered
and resumed his literary and political work with renewed
vigour. After *Le Temps d'éborde* (1947) (Time Overflows), he
published *Poèmes politiques* (Political Poems) in 1948 and *Une
leçon de morale* (A Lesson in Morality) in 1949. In the former
he spoke, simply and movingly as usual, of his solidarity
with the fighters for freedom in France and in the world. In
the latter, each poem put forward contrasting views of man,
the bad side and the good side. He explained in his preface
that *'le mal doit être mis au bien'* (evil must be turned into good)
and added: 'Even if in the whole of my life I had known but
one moment of hope, I would have waged this fight. Even if
I am to lose it, for others will win it. All others.'

Apart from work and companionship, what helped
Eluard to recover was the fact that he went to Mexico in
1949, in order to attend a congress of the World Peace
Council and returned with a young French woman he had
met there, Dominique Lemor. She became his third wife,
and the 1951 collection of poems he dedicated to her was
significantly called *Le Phénix* (The Phoenix) to show that, like

the legendary bird, he had come back to life out of his deepest grief. In the poem, *Dominique aujourd'hui présente* (Dominique Present Today), he wrote:

Tu es venue j'étais très triste j'ai dit oui
C'est à partir de toi que j'ai dit oui au monde

You came I was very sad I said yes
It was from the time I met you that I said yes to the world

In 1951, he also published *Pouvoir tout dire* (Being Able to Say Everything), in which he put forward his aim of embracing the whole of reality. Both the title and the aim represented the liberation he had already foreseen in 1938 when he wrote a poem to André Breton about *Quelques mots qui, jusqu'ici, m'étaient mystérieusement interdits* (A Few Words Which, Hitherto, I Had Mysteriously Been Forbidden to Use). Prophetically, the poem ended with the following lines:

Mots que j'écris ici
Contre toute évidence
Avec le grand souci
De tout dire

Words which I write here
Against all evidence
With my great care being
To say everything

In November 1952, Eluard died of a heart attack, having expressed in his last poem, *Le Château des pauvres* (The Castle of the Poor), his boundless faith in youth and in the future:

L'horizon s'offre à la sagesse
Le coeur aux yeux de la jeunesse

19

Tout monte rien ne se retire

The horizon unfolds before wisdom
The heart before the eyes of youth
Everything rises nothing recedes

A year after his death, the last collection of his poems was published, *Poésie ininterrompue II*. It included *Le Château des pauvres* and also a poem entitled *Abolir les mystères* (Abolishing Mysteries), from which the following lines may be regarded as his poetic and human testament:

Il faut entre nos mains qui sont les plus nombreuses
Broyer la mort idiote abolir les mystères
Construire la raison de naître et vivre heureux

We must with our hands which are the most numerous
Pulverize senseless death abolish mysteries
Build the reason for being born and live happy

A great poet does not really need lengthy introductions or sophisticated commentaries in order to be appreciated. This is especially true of Eluard, whose poetry is that of the real world. To anyone who has but a drop of 'the milk of human kindness', i.e. to anyone who feels a sense of kinship in the world of fellow human beings, the voice of Eluard will sound like the voice of a close friend. All the same, a few words concerning his versification, his imagery and his main themes may help to add to our enjoyment by providing a number of simple, easily recognisable guidelines. The chief characteristic of Eluard's poetic technique is the great variety of metres he uses; some are fairly common among French poets, others less so. He refuses to be the slave of any one metre, always choosing a rhythmic structure which is adapted to the content of his poem and which relies on the positioning of key words in order to emphasise or clarify the meaning. It is often assumed that Eluard spurns the alexandrine on principle as being too formal and too traditional, but this is not really true. Apart from the fact that in the twenties, his surrealist friends used to chaff him for his 'unorthodox' interest in the alexandrine, it so happens that this particular metre occurs time and again in his poems, from the 1924 *L'égalité des sexes* (The Equality of the Sexes) in *Mourir de ne pas mourir*, which is made up of three quatrains in alexandrines, to the 1951 poem, *Tout dire*, which is made up of twenty-three quatrains and uses no other metre throughout. To Eluard, the alexandrine was neither a must nor a taboo, it was, like all other metres, a metre to be used when the occasion required it. Neither is it quite correct to regard Eluard as opposed to rhymes as such, even though he once told Yves Sandre that 'the rhyme is dangerous because it lulls you to sleep.' For here again, it is the content which decides whether rhymes would add to or detract from the overall idea which the poet wishes to convey.

Another important feature of Eluard's poetry is that he never, or very seldom, uses punctuation. Here he merely follows Apollinaire, and for the same reason, believing that in a poem, punctuation is unnecessary, because the rhythm and the sense create their own natural punctuation. Unlike Apollinaire, however, Eluard does not rely on the lack of punctuation to make his verse ambiguous and capable of more than one interpretation, but rather to increase the self-evident meaning of what he is trying to say. A number of students who read Eluard for the first time were somewhat surprised to be told that he does not use punctuation — they themselves had not even noticed it, so compelling was the inner logic and the structure of what the poet had to say. One device which helps to forget the absence of punctuation is the skilful use of repetition. Sometimes, an expression regularly occurs at the beginning of each line, such as the *Que voulez-vous* in *Couvre-feu*, sometimes, it is found, no less regularly, at the end of each stanza, as is the case with *J'écris ton nom* in *Liberté*. These repetitions carry the reader or the hearer away and create their own atmosphere, an atmosphere which varies with each poem; it ranges from incantation to strking antithesis, from the music of a soothing lullaby to the indignation at the sight of injustice and cruelty.

With regard to imagery, it is characterised by its appeal to the senses and the importance of concrete objects and of everyday things. For Eluard, to be wholly part of the world, the world of matter and the world of men, meant above all to experience the former to the full, and to share with the inhabitants of the latter the most natural, most common-place sensations and feelings. This explains why he was able to invest almost anything with a poetic quality. In this respect, the poem, *Gabriel Péri*, is not only a tribute to a martyr of the Resistance, it is also in part a kind of *Ars Poetica*, of which the golden rule is that the simplest of words are those which are the real texture of life, and consequently of poetry:

> Il y a des mots qui font vivre
> Et ce sont des mots innocents

It was once said of Racine that the secret of his effective imagery was that he almost did away with images. The same might be said of Eluard, for his images are the very opposite of refined metaphors, they belong to life as we know it. No wonder that Gaston Bachelard was able to say that in Eluard's poetry, 'images are right': they do not take us away from reality, they rather plunge us straight into it. It is significant that the poet seldom uses similes: to him, happiness is not *like* the light, it *is* the light:

> Que le bonheur soit la lumière

It is equally significant that he is so fond of personification. He speaks, for example, of

> Une tranquille rue rouillée
> Qui n'a jamais été jeune

A quiet rusty street
That was never young

thus endowing the street with character, colour and old age.
Eluard's favourite images are drawn from the human body,
from nature, and from familiar surroundings. A good
illustration of the 'basic' character of his poetry is the
importance of the four elements, fire and water in the first
place, and air and earth to a lesser extent. Sometimes, an
image is quite unexpected, as is the case in the line,

La terre est bleue comme une orange

The earth is blue like an orange

but this is neither gratuitous nor a piece of utter nonsense:
the earth is indeed like an orange because it is round, and
an orange can turn blue when it is mouldy.

A clue to Eluard's approach to poetic style and imagery is
provided by what he says in *Les sentiers et les routes de la poésie*
(The Paths and the Roads of Poetry), a book which came out
in 1952 and is made up of five radio talks he gave in 1949.
Two statements stand out. The first one asserts that 'nothing
is more horrible than poeticised language, than words
which are too nice and are gracefully linked to other pearls.
Genuine poetry includes coarse nudity, anchors which are
not the sheet-anchors of last hope, tears which are not
rainbow-hued . . . *For poetry is in life*.' In the second one, we
read that the real poet eagerly listens to the 'obscure news of
the world' which is supplied by 'grass, pebbles, dirt,
splendours', and that his task is to convey all the delights of
language, the language of 'the man in the street' and 'the
sage', the language 'of a woman, a child, a lunatic'. The man
who uttered these words was no longer a surrealist, yet as he
spoke in this vein, he was truer than ever to the ideals of his
youth. For it was one of the surrealists' ambitions to give
poetry the aim and the content which Lautréamont had in
mind when he said that the goal of poetry was practical

truth ('*La poésie doit avoir pour but la vérité practique*') and that it should be made by all, not by one person ('*La poésie doit être faite par tous, non par un*').

Finally, the main themes which are found in Eluard's poetry are love, brotherhood and kindness. The first one is to be expected from most poets. Eluard's originality, which he shares with Aragon, is that he is the poet of the couple. In this respect, his sense of genuine love and his sense of human solidarity are complementary, for the couple is the first step towards a society of brotherhood. When he took part in a surrealist questionnaire in the twenties, one of the questions that was put to him was: what do you think of a man who betrays his beliefs in order to please the woman he loves? This is what he replied: 'The cause which I defend is also the cause of love. To demand such a token from an honest man can only destroy his love or lead to his death.' Eluard looked upon love as providing physical pleasure and human warmth, and above all as the antidote to loneliness. In the following lines, which succintly sum up his approach, love and commitment are inextricably linked (the lines come from *Notre vie*, the last poem in *Le Temps déborde*):

> Nous n'irons plus au but un par un mais par deux
> Nous connaissant par deux nous nous connaîtrons tous
> Nous nous aimerons tous et nos enfants riront
> Da la légende noire où pleure un solitaire

> We shall not reach the goal one by one but in twos
> Knowing each other in twos we shall all know one
>   another
> We shall all love one another and our children will
>   laugh
> At the sombre legend in which a lonely man is weeping

The couple being the embryonic form of humanity reconciled with itself, Eluard could declare in 1947 that 'to love is our only reason for living.' One can distinguish three love cycles in his life and in his poetry: the Gala cycle (1913-1929), in which love is youthful, pure, idealised and self-absorbing; the Nusch cycle (1929-1946), in which love gradually takes on the form of the highest form of human communication, a fact eloquently illustrated by the increasing use of *'nous'* (we, us) instead of *'je'* (I); and the Dominique cycle (1949-1952) in which the love of the elderly poet for a young woman restores both his confidence and his resolve to contribute to the happiness of others.

The theme of brotherhood is an extension of love. Loving a woman and loving his fellow human beings were to Eluard part of the same process of overcoming solitude. In the 1948 preface to the *Poèmes politiques*, he summed up his own personal and intellectual development as an evolution:

De l'horizon d'un seul à l'horizon de tous

From the horizon of a single man to the horizon of all

Both his surrealism and his communism must be seen as attempts to be at one with other people, to share their dreams and their yearnings for happiness. One of his favourite images was the use of the intimate pronoun *'tu'* in order to express kinship, as this is reserved for close friends. The highest tribute he could pay Péri was to call him a friend, *'tutoyons-le'*, and the supreme lesson of the martyr's death in his eyes was that all men should be friends, *'tutoyons-nous'*. Some people may regret the fact that his ideal of brotherhood should have led him to political involvement, but this must be seen as part of Eluard's realism: he knew that mere declarations were not enough, that purely individual gestures were limited, and that it was by reorganising society that one could lay the basis for genuine human solidarity. One need not share his political beliefs in order to respect the sincerity of his commitment and the humanitarian motives which were responsible for it.

25

The last theme which deserves a brief mention is kindness. This makes him almost unique among poets, at any rate among his contemporaries, if one excepts Bertolt Brecht. The other surrealists and the other committed writers of his generation were more violent, more impatient, more intolerant than he. Although in the great majority of cases, their love for humanity was genuine and deep, it was not accompanied by the gentleness which characterises Eluard. Aragon, for example, wrote movingly about the French women who had been tortured in the Auschwitz concentration camp; could he also have written the poem in which Eluard expressed his sorrow at the sight of a woman ill-treated by an angry crowd because she had slept with German soldiers? He might have agreed with his friend that she was far less guilty than the real 'collaborators', but only Eluard could have found it in his heart to call her a victim who was unaware of what she was doing. Although far from being a Christian, the poet could have paraphased Christ and told his countrymen: 'Forgive her, for she knows not what she does.' All the same, again like Christ, and indeed like all great moral reformers, he never allowed his kindness to extend to the tyrants, the executioners and the torturers. His kindness was allied to a great sense of justice, and without any trace of petty vindictiveness, he could calmly assert that

Il n'y a pas de matin plus éclatant
Que le matin où les traîtres succombent
Il n'y a pas de salut sur la terre
Tant que l'on peut pardonner aux bourreaux

There is no dawn more glorious
Than the dawn when traitors fall
There is no salvation on earth
So long as torturers are forgiven

One of the most revealing signs of his evolution as a man and as a poet is provided by the three *Critique de la poésie* which he wrote. The first one, which is part of the 1932 *La vie immédiate*, aggressively asserts that the finest poems are those which denounce 'the reign of the bourgeois, the reign of coppers and priests'; the second one, included in the 1942 *Poésie et vérité*, and still called a 'critique' of poetry, is neither aggressive nor polemical: it contrasts all that is good and beautiful in life with the cruelty that led to the killing and torture of great artists — Garcia Lorca, Saint-Pol Roux and Decour —; the final one, entitled *La poésie doit avoir pour but la vérité pratique*, and included in the *Poèmes politiques*, represents the final 'critique' of poetry: in it, Eluard replies to his 'exacting friends' who are unwilling and unable to follow him whenever he sings of his 'whole street'; he tells them that he, for his part, has discovered that the great secret of genuine poetry is the knowledge that men

Ont besoin d'être unis d'espérer de lutter
Pour expliquer le monde et pour le transformer

Need to be united to hope to struggle
In order to explain the world and to change it

Max Adereth
University of Lancaster

27

ELUARD
SELECTED POEMS

CINQ HAI-KAIS

Le vent
Hésitant
Roule une cigarette d'air.

La muette parle
C'est l'imperfection de l'art
Ce langage obscur.

L'automobile est vraiment lancée
Quatre têtes de martyrs
Roulent sous les roues.

Ah! mille flammes, un feu, la lumière,
Une ombre!
Le soleil me suit.

Une plume donne au chapeau
Un air de légèreté
La cheminée fume.

FIVE HAIKU

The wind,
Undecided,
Rolls a cigarette of air

The dumb girl talks:
It is art's imperfection,
This impenetrable speech.

The motor car is truly launched:
Four martyrs' heads
Roll under the wheels.

Ah! a thousand flames, a fire,
The light, a shadow!
The sun is following me.

A feather gives to a hat
A touch of lightness:
The chimney smokes.

1920

FUIR

L'araignée rapide,
Pieds et mains de la peur,
Est arrivée.

L'araignée,
Heureuse de son poids,
Reste immobile
Comme le plomb du fil à plomb.

Et quand elle repart,
Brisant tous les fils,
C'est la poursuite dans le vide
Qu'il faut imaginer,

Toute chose détruite.

FLIGHT

The quick spider,
Feet and hands of dread,
Is here.

The spider,
Happy with its weight,
Stays motionless
Like the lead of the plumb-line.

And when it runs away,
Breaking all the threads,
It is pursuit into nothingness
You must imagine,

All else destroyed.

1920

OUVRIER

Voir des planches dans les arbres,
Des chemins dans les montagnes,
Au bel âge, à l'âge de force,
Tisser du fer et pétrir de la pierre,
Embellir la nature,
La nature sans sa parure,
Travailler.

WORKER

Seeing timber in the trees,
Roads into the mountains,
In the days of youth, days of strength,
Bending iron and shaping stone,
Adorning nature,
Nature without her dress,
I work.

1921

NUDITÉ DE LA VÉRITÉ

Je le sais bien.

Le désespoir n'a pas d'ailes,
L'amour non plus,
Pas de visage,
Ne parlent pas,
Je ne bouge pas,
Je ne les regarde pas,
Je ne leur parle pas
Mais je suis bien aussi vivant que mon amour et que mon
    désespoir.

THE NAKEDNESS OF TRUTH

I know it well.

Despair has no wings,
Nor has love,
No countenance:
They do not speak.
I do not stir,
I do not behold them,
I do not speak to them,
But I am as real as my love and my despair.

1924

L'AMOUREUSE

Elle est debout sur mes paupières
Et ses cheveux sont dans les miens,
Elle a la forme de mes mains,
Elle a la couleur de mes yeux,
Elle s'engloutit dans mon ombre
Comme une pierre sur le ciel.

Elle a toujours les yeux ouverts
Et ne me laisse pas dormir.
Ses rêves en pleine lumière
Font s'évaporer les soleils,
Me font rire, pleurer et rire,
Parler sans avoir rien à dire.

WOMAN IN LOVE

She is standing on my eyes
And her hair is in my hair;
She has the figure of my hands
And the colour of my sight.
She is swallowed in my shade
Like a stone against the sky.

She will never close her eyes
And will never let me sleep;
And her dreams in day's full light
Make the suns evaporate,
Make me laugh and cry and laugh,
Speak when I have nought to say.

1924

39

PAR UNE NUIT NOUVELLE

Femme avec laquelle j'ai vécu
Femme avec laquelle je vis
Femme avec laquelle je vivrai
Toujours la même
Il te faut un manteau rouge
Des gants rouges un masque rouge
Et des bas noirs
Des raisons des preuves
De te voir toute nue
Nudité pure ô parure parée

Seins ô mon cœur

ON A NEW NIGHT

Woman with whom I have lived,
Woman with whom I live,
Woman with whom I shall live;
The same woman always,
You must have a red cloak,
Red gloves, a red mask,
And black stockings:
Reasons, proofs
For seeing you quite naked;
Unsullied nakedness, O adorning dress!

Breasts, O my heart!

1932

ÊTRE

Le front comme un drapeau perdu
Je te traîne quand je suis seul
Dans des rues froides
Des chambres noires
En criant misère

Je ne veux pas les lâcher
Tes mains claires et compliquées
Nées dans le miroir clos des miennes

Tout le reste est parfait
Tout le reste est encore plus inutile
Que la vie

Creuse la terre sous ton ombre

Une nappe d'eau près des seins
Où se noyer
Comme une pierre

BEING

My brow a surrendered flag
I drag you by the hands when I am lonely
In cold streets
Dark rooms
Crying want

I will not let them go
Your intricate light hands
Born in the darkened mirror of my own

All else is perfect
All else is vainer still
Than life

Dig the earth under your shadow

A sheet of water near your breasts
Where I can sink
Like a stone

1936

ÉPITAPHE D'UN AGRICULTEUR ESPAGNOL

Le général Franco m'a enrôlé pour devenir maudit
soldat,
Je n'ai pas déserté, j'avais peur, voyez-vous, on m'aurait
fusillé,
J'avais peur — c'est pourquoi, dans l'armée, j'ai lutté
contre le droit, contre la liberté,
Sous les murs d'Irún. Et la mort m'a quand même
rejoint.

EPITAPH FOR A SPANISH PEASANT

General Franco enlisted me
So I became a wretched soldier.
I did not desert,
I was afraid, you see, they would have shot me.
I was afraid, which is why, in the army,
I fought against freedom, against justice,
Under the walls of Irun.
But death caught up with me just the same.

1936

NOVEMBRE 1936

Regardez travailler les bâtisseurs de ruines
Ils sont riches patients ordonnés noirs et bêtes
Mais ils font de leur mieux pour être seuls sur terre
Ils sont au bord de l'homme et le comblent d'ordures
Ils plient au ras du sol des palais sans cervelle.

On s'habitue à tout
Sauf à ces oiseux de plomb
Sauf à leur haine de ce qui brille
Sauf à leur céder la place.

Parlez du ciel le ciel se vide
L'automne nous importe peu
Nos maîtres ont tapé du pied
Nous avons oublié l'automne
Et nous oublierons nos maîtres.

Ville en baisse océan fait d'une goutte d'eau sauvée
D'un seul diamant cultivé au grand jour
Madrid ville habituelle à ceux qui ont souffert
De cet épouvantable bien qui nie être en exemple
Qui ont souffert
De la misère indispensable à l'éclat de ce bien.

Que la bouche remonte vers sa vérité
Souffle rare sourire comme une chaîne brisée
Que l'homme délivré de son passé absurde
Dresse devant son frère un visage semblable

Et donne à la raison des ailes vagabondes.

NOVEMBER 1936

Look the builders of ruins are working
They are rich patient tidy dark and ugly
But they do their best to stay alone on earth
Detached from man they heap the dirt upon him
Without a mind they fold up mansions flat.

One gets used to everything
Except these leaden birds
Except their hatred of shining things
Except making way for them.

Speak of the sky the sky empties
Autumn does not matter much
Our masters stamped their feet
We forgot autumn
And we shall forget our masters.

A city declining an ocean made of a drop of water spared
Made of a single diamond cut in broad daylight
Madrid a city familiar to those who suffered
From this frightful blessing that denies example
Who suffered
From the torment that the lustre of this blessing needs.

Let the mouth return towards its truth
Whisper rare smile like a broken chain
Let man delivered of his senseless past
Rise before his brother a friendly face

And give to reason roving wings.

1936

47

SŒURS D'ESPÉRANCE

Sœurs d'espérance ô femmes courageuses
Contre la mort vous avez fait un pacte
Celui d'unir les vertus de l'amour

Ô mes sœurs survivantes
Vous jouez votre vie
Pour que la vie triomphe

Le jour est proche ô mes sœurs de grandeur
Où nous rirons des mots guerre et misère
Rien ne tiendra de ce qui fut douleur

Chaque visage aura droit aux caresses.

SISTERS OF HOPE

Sisters of hope O courageous women
Against death you made a covenant
Joining together all love's goodnesses

O my triumphant sisters
You stake your lives
That life may overcome

The day is near O my sisters of grandeur
When we shall laugh at words like war and pain
And nothing shall be left of what was sorrow

Every face shall have a right to kisses.

1936

ON NE PEUT ME CONNAÎTRE

On ne peut me connaître
Mieux que tu me connais

Tes yeux dans lesquels nous dormons
Tous les deux
Ont fait à mes lumières d'homme
Un sort meilleur qu'aux nuits du monde

Tes yeux dans lesquels je voyage
Ont donné aux gestes des routes
Un sens détaché de la terre

Dans tes yeux ceux qui nous révèlent
Notre solitude infinie
Ne sont plus ce qu'ils croyaient être

On ne peut te connaître
Mieux que je te connais.

I CANNOT BE KNOWN

I cannot be known
Better than you know me

Your eyes in which we sleep
We together
Have made for my man's gleam
A better fate than for the common nights

Your eyes in which I travel
Have given to the signs along the roads
A meaning alien to the earth

In your eyes those who reveal to us
Our endless solitude
Are no longer what they thought themselves to be

You cannot be known
Better than I know you.

1936

LA VICTOIRE DE GUERNICA

I

Beau monde des masures
De la mine et des champs

II

Visages bons au feu visages bons au froid
Aux refus à la nuit aux injures aux coups

III

Visages bons à tout
Voici le vide qui vous fixe
Votre mort va servir d'exemple

IV

La mort cœur renversé

V

Ils vous ont fait payer le pain
Le ciel la terre l'eau le sommeil
Et la misère
De votre vie

VI

Ils disaient désirer la bonne intelligence
Ils rationnaient les forts jugeaient les fous
Faisaient l'aumône partageaient un sou en deux
Ils saluaient les cadavres
Ils s'accablaient de politesses

VII

Ils persévèrent ils exagèrent ils ne sont pas de notre monde

THE VICTORY OF GUERNICA

I

Fair world of hovel
Mine and field.

II

Faces fit for burning faces fit for freezing
For denial for darkness for insults blows

III

Faces fit for anything
Here is emptiness that stares at you
Your death will serve as an example.

IV

Death a heart cast down.

V

They made you pay for bread
For sky earth water sleep
And for the poverty
Of your lives.

VI

They said they wanted good relations
They rationed the strong passed judgment on the mad
Gave alms split a penny in two
They saluted corpses
Heaped courtesies on one another.

VII

They try hard they overdo it they are not of our kind.

VIII

Les femmes les enfants ont le même trésor
De feuilles vertes de printemps et de lait pur
Et de durée
Dans leurs yeux purs

IX

Les femmes les enfants ont le même trésor
Dans les yeux
Les hommes le défendent comme ils peuvent

X

Les femmes les enfants ont les mêmes roses rouges
Dans les yeux
Chacun montre son sang

XI

La peur et le courage de vivre et de mourir
La mort si difficile et si facile

XII

Hommes pour qui ce trésor fut chanté
Hommes pour qui ce trésor fut gâché

XIII

Hommes réels pour qui le désespoir
Alimente le feu dévorant de l'espoir
Ouvrons ensemble le dernier bourgeon de l'avenir

XIV

Parias la mort la terre et la hideur
De nos ennemis ont la couleur
Monotone de notre nuit
Nous en aurons raison.

VIII

Women and children have the same riches
Of green leaves spring and pure milk
And endurance
In their pure eyes.

IX

Women and children have the same riches
In their eyes
Men defend them as they can.

X

Women and children have the same red roses
In their eyes
They show each their blood.

XI

The fear and the courage to live and to die
Death so difficult and so easy.

XII

Men for whom these riches were extolled
Men for whom these riches were debased.

XIII

True men for whom despair
Feeds the devouring fire of hope
Let us open together the last bud of the future.

XIV

Outcasts the death the ground the hideous sight
Of our enemies have the dull
Colour of our night
Despite them we shall overcome.

1937

LES MAINS LIBRES

Le Désir

Jeunesse du fauve
Bonheur en sang
Dans un bassin de lait.

Le Tournant

J'espère
Ce qui m'est interdit.

Burlesque

Fille de glace donne-moi
Confiance en moi.

L'angoisse et L'inquiétude

Purifier raréfier stériliser détruire
Semer multiplier alimenter détruire.

Les Mains Libres

Cette averse est un feu de paille
La chaleur va l'étouffer.

from FREE HANDS

Desire

The beast's young urgency,
Happiness in blood
In a pool of milk.

The Corner

I hope to find
What is denied to me.

Burlesque

Girl of ice, give to me
Confidence in myself.

Anguish and Anxiety

Purify rarify cleanse destroy
Sow multiply feed destroy.

Free Hands

This shower of rain is a burst of fire:
The heat will smother it.

Le vent est à la barre
L'horizon vertical
Verse le ciel dans ta main maladroite.

The Broken Mirror

The wind is steering;
The vertical horizon
Pours the sky into your nervous hand.

1937

L'ABSENCE

Je te parle à travers les villes
Je te parle à travers les plaines

Ma bouche est sur ton oreiller

Les deux faces des murs font face
A ma voix qui te reconnaît

Je te parle d'éternité

Ô villes souvenirs de villes
Villes drapées dans nos désirs
Villes précoces et tardives
Villes fortes villes intimes
Dépouillées de tous leurs maçons
De leurs penseurs de leurs fantômes

Campagne règle d'émeraude
Vive vivante survivante
Le blé du ciel sur notre terre
Nourrit ma voix je rêve et pleure
Je ris et rêve entre les flammes
Entre les grappes du soleil

Et sur mon corps ton corps étend
La nappe de son miroir clair.

ABSENCE

I speak to you across cities
I speak to you across plains

My mouth is upon your pillow

Both faces of the walls come meeting
My voice discovering you

I speak to you of all seasons

O cities memories of cities
Cities wrapped in our desires
Cities come early cities come lately
Cities strong and cities secret
Plundered of their master builders
All their thinkers all their ghosts

Fields pattern of emerald
Bright living surviving
The harvest of the sky over our earth
Feeds my voice I dream and weep
I laugh and dream among the flames
Among the clusters of the sun

And over my body your body spreads
The sheet of its bright mirror.

1942

COURAGE

Paris a froid Paris a faim
Paris ne mange plus de marrons dans la rue
Paris a mis de vieux vêtements de vieille
Paris dort tout debout sans air dans le métro
Plus de malheur encore est imposé aux pauvres
Et la sagesse et la folie
De Paris malheureux
C'est l'air pur c'est le feu
C'est la beauté c'est la bonté
De ses travailleurs affamés
Ne crie pas au secours Paris
Tu es vivant d'une vie sans égale
Et derrière la nudité
De ta pâleur de ta maigreur
Tout ce qui est humain se révèle en tes yeux
Paris ma belle ville
Fine comme une aiguille forte comme une épée
Ingénue et savante
Tu ne supportes pas l'injustice
Pour toi c'est le seul désordre
Tu vas te libérer Paris
Paris tremblant comme une étoile
Notre espoir survivant
Tu vas te libérer de la fatigue et de la boue
Frères ayons du courage
Nous qui ne sommes pas casqués
Ni bottés ni gantés ni bien élevés
Un rayon s'allume en nos veines
Notre lumière nous revient
Les meilleurs d'entre nous sont morts pour nous
Et voici que leur sang retrouve notre cœur
Et c'est de nouveau le matin un matin de Paris
La pointe de la délivrance
L'espace du printemps naissant
La force idiote a le dessous

COURAGE

Paris is cold Paris is hungry
Paris no longer eats chestnuts in the streets
Paris has put on an old woman's old clothes
Paris sleeps standing airless in the Metro
More misery still is heaped upon the poor
And the wisdom and the folly
Of unhappy Paris
Are the fire and the pure air
Are the beauty and the goodness
Of her hungry toilers
Do not cry for help Paris
You are alive with a life without equal
And behind the bareness
Of your pallor and your thinness
All that is human is revealed in your eyes
Paris my handsome city
Sharp as a needle strong as a sword
Artless and erudite
You do not bear injustice
For you it is the only chaos
You will free yourself Paris
Paris twinkling like a star
Our surviving hope
You will free yourself from dirt and weariness
Brothers let us have courage
We who are not helmeted
Nor booted nor gloved nor well brought up
A ray lights up in our veins
Our light comes back to us
The best of us have died for us
And their blood now finds again our hearts
And it is morning once more a Paris morning
The dawn of deliverance
The space of spring new born
Senseless force has the worst of it

Ces esclaves nos ennemis
S'ils ont compris
S'ils sont capables de comprendre
Vont se lever

These slaves our enemies
If they have understood
If they are capable of understanding
Will rise up.

1942

LA DERNIÈRE NUIT

I

Ce petit monde meurtrier
Est orienté vers l'innocent
Lui ôte le pain de la bouche
Et donne sa maison au feu
Lui prend sa veste et ses souliers
Lui prend son temps et ses enfants

Ce petit monde meurtrier
Confond les morts et les vivants
Blanchit la boue gracie les traîtres
Transforme la parole en bruit

Merci minuit douze fusils
Rendent la paix à l'innocent
Et c'est aux foules d'enterrer
Sa chair sanglante et son ciel noir
Et c'est aux foules de comprendre
La faiblesse des meurtriers.

II

Le prodige serait une légère poussée contre le mur
Ce serait de pouvoir cette poussière

Ce serait d'être unis.

III

Ils avaient mis à vif ses mains courbé son dos
Ils avaient creusé un trou dans sa tête
Et pour mourir il avait dû souffrir
Toute sa vie.

THE LAST NIGHT

I

This murderous little world
Is aimed at the simple man
It snatches the bread from his mouth
And delivers his house to fire
Steals his coat and his shoes
Steals his time and his children

This murderous little world
Confuses the dead and the living
Whitens mud and forgives traitors
And turns the word to noise

Thank you midnight twelve rifles
Return peace to the simple man
And now the crowds must bury
His bloodshot flesh and his dark sky
And now the crowds must understand
The weakness of murderers.

II

The wonder would be a slight push against the wall
The power to shake off this dust

To be united.

III

They had slashed his hands bent his back
They had dug a hole in his head
And to die he had to suffer
All his life.

IV

Beauté créée pour les heureux
Beauté tu cours un grand danger

Ces mains croisées sur tes genoux
Sont les outils d'un assassin

Cette bouche chantant très haut
Sert de sébile au mendiant

Et cette coupe de lait pur
Devient le sein d'une putain.

V

Les pauvres ramassaient leur pain dans le ruisseau
Leur regard couvrait la lumière
Et ils n'avaient plus peur la nuit

Très faibles leur faiblesse les faisait sourire
Dans le fond de leur ombre ils emportaient leur corps
Ils ne se voyaient plus qu'à travers leur détresse
Ils ne se servaient plus que d'un langage intime
Et j'entendais parler doucement prudemment
D'un ancien espoir grand comme la main

J'entendais calculer
Les dimensions multipliées de la feuille d'automne
La fonte de la vague au sein de la mer calme
J'entendais calculer
Les dimensions multipliées de la force future.

IV

Beauty created for the happy
Beauty you run a great risk

These hands crossed on your knees
Are an assassin's implements

This mouth singing aloud
Serves as a beggar's bowl

And this cup of pure milk
Becomes the breast of a whore.

V

The poor picked their bread from the gutter
Their stare spread over the light
In the dark they were no more afraid

So weak their weakness made them smile
In the depth of shadows they bore away their bodies
They saw each other only through distress
They used only a secret language
And I heard them speak softly carefully
Of an old hope as big as a hand

I heard them calculate
The multiplied dimensions of the autumn leaf
The melting of the wave on the crest of the quiet sea
I heard them calculate
The multiplied dimensions of future strength.

VI

Je suis né derrière une façade affreuse
J'ai mangé j'ar ri j'ai rêvé j'ai eu honte
J'ai vécu comme une ombre
Et pourtant j'ai su chanter le soleil
Le soleil entier celui qui respire
Dans chaque poitrine et dans tous les yeux
La goutte de candeur qui luit après les larmes.

VII

Nous jetons le fagot des ténèbres au feu
Nous brisons les serrures rouillées de l'injustice
Des hommes vont venir qui n'ont plus peur d'eux-
mêmes
Car ils sont sûrs de tous les hommes
Car l'ennemi à figure d'homme disparaît.

VI

I was born behind a hideous facade
I have eaten I have laughed I have dreamed I have been
  ashamed
I have lived like a shadow
Yet I have known how to extol the sun
The whole sun which breathes
In every breast and in all eyes
The drop of candour which shines after tears.

VII

We throw the faggots of darkness on the fire
We smash the rusty locks of injustice
Men will come no longer fearing themselves
For they are sure of all men
For the enemy with a man's face disappears.

1942

LIBERTÉ

Sur mes cahiers d'écolier
Sur mon pupitre et les arbres
Sur le sable sur la neige
J'écris ton nom

Sur toutes les pages lues
Sur toutes les pages blanches
Pierre sang papier ou cendre
J'écris ton nom

Sur les images dorées
Sur les armes des guerriers
Sur la couronne des rois
J'écris ton nom

Sur la jungle et le désert
Sur les nids sur les genêts
Sur l'écho de mon enfance
J'écris ton nom

Sur les merveilles des nuits
Sur le pain blanc des journées
Sur les saisons fiancées
J'écris ton nom

Sur tous mes chiffons d'azur
Sur l'étang soleil moisi
Sur le lac lune vivante
J'écris ton nom

Sur les champs sur l'horizon
Sur les ailes des oiseaux
Et sur le moulin des ombres
J'écris ton nom

LIBERTY

On my schoolboy's copy-books
On my desk and on the trees
On sand and snow
I write your name

On all pages read
On all blank pages
Stone blood paper or ash
I write your name

On the gilded images
On the arms of warriors
On the crown of kings
I write your name

On the jungle and the desert
On nests on gorse
On the echo of my childhood
I write your name

On the wonders of the nights
On the white bread of the days
On seasons betrothed
I write your name

On all my rags of blue
On the pond musty sun
On the lake living moon
I write your name

On the fields on the horizon
On the wings of birds
And on the mill of shadows
I write your name

Sur chaque bouffée d'aurore
Sur la mer sur les bateaux
Sur la montagne démente
J'écris ton nom

Sur la mousse des nuages
Sur les sueurs de l'orage
Sur la pluie épaisse et fade
J'écris ton nom

Sur les formes scintillantes
Sur les cloches des couleurs
Sur la vérité physique
J'écris ton nom

Sur les sentiers éveillés
Sur les routes déployées
Sur les places qui débordent
J'écris ton nom

Sur la lampe qui s'allume
Sur la lampe qui s'éteint
Sur mes maisons réunies
J'écris ton nom

Sur le fruit coupé en deux
Du miroir et de ma chambre
Sur mon lit coquille vide
J'écris ton nom

Sur mon chien gourmand et tendre
Sur ses oreilles dressées
Sur sa patte maladriote
J'écris ton nom

On every whiff of daybreak
On sea on ships
On the raging mountain
I write your name

On the foam of clouds
On the toil of storm
On the dense and tasteless rain
I write your name

On gleaming shapes
On bells of colour
On physical truth
I write your name

On awakened paths
On roads spread out
On overflowing squares
I write your name

On the lamp that kindles
On the lamp that dies
On my houses joined together
I write your name

On the fruit cut in two
By the mirror and my room
On my bed empty shell
I write your name

On my greedy loving dog
On his pricked up ears
On his awkward paw
I write your name

Sur le tremplin de ma porte
Sur les objets familiers
Sur le flot du feu béni
J'écris ton nom

Sur toute chair accordée
Sur le font de mes amis
Sur chaque main qui se tend
J'écris ton nom

Sur la vitre des surprises
Sur les lèvres attentives
Bien au-dessus du silence
J'écris ton nom

Sur mes refuges détruits
Sur mes phares écroulés
Sur les murs de mon ennui
J'écris ton nom

Sur l'absence sans désir
Sur la solitude nue
Sur les marches de la mort
J'écris ton nom

Sur la santé revenue
Sur le risque disparu
Sur l'espoir sans souvenir
J'écris ton nom

Et par le pouvoir d'un mot
Je recommence ma vie
Je suis né pour te connaître
Pour te nommer

Liberté

On the threshold of my door
On familiar things
On the surge of blessed fire
I write your name

On all accordant flesh
On the foreheads of my friends
On every hand held out
I write your name

On the window of surprises
On attentive lips
High above the silence
I write your name

On my devastated shelters
On my perished beacons
On the walls of my fatigue
I write your name

On absence without desire
On barren solitude
On the steps of death
I write your name

On health returned
On vanished risk
On hope without remembrance
I write your name

And by the power of a word
I begin my life again
I was born to know you
To name you

Liberty.

1942

LES SEPT POÈMES
D'AMOUR EN GUERRE

J'écris dans ce pays où l'on parque les hommes
Dans l'ordure et la soif, le silence et la faim . . .

François la Colère (*Le Musée Grévin*).

I

Un navire dans tes yeux
Se rendait maître du vent
Tes yeux étaient le pays
Que l'on retrouve en un instant

Patients tes yeux nous attendaient

Sous les arbres des forêts
Dans la pluie dans la tourmente
Sur la neige des sommets
Entre les yeux et les jeux des enfants

Patients tes yeux nous attendaient

Ils étaient une vallée
Plus tendre qu'un seul brin d'herbe
Leur soleil donnait du poids
Aux maigres moissons humaines

Nous attendaient pour nous voir
Toujours
Car nous apportions l'amour
La jeunesse de l'amour
Et la raison de l'amour
La sagesse de l'amour
Et l'immortalité

SEVEN POEMS OF LOVE AT WAR

I write in that land where men are herded
into filth and thirst, silence and hunger...

François la Colère* (*La Musée Grévin*)

I

Your eyes were a ship
A ship lord of the wind
And your eyes were a land
Found again in an instant

Patient your eyes awaited us

Under the forest trees
In rain in tempest
On the snow of mountain tops
In the eyes and games of children

Patient your eyes awaited us

They were a valley
Softer than a single blade of grass
Their sun nourished
The lean human years

Waited to see us
Always
For we bore love
The youth of love
And the meaning of love
The wisdom of love
And immortality.

*Pseudonym of Louis Aragon while he was in the Resistance.

II

Jour de nos yeux mieux peuplés
Que les plus grandes batailles

Villes et banlieues villages
De nos yeux vainqueurs du temps

Dans la fraîche vallée brûle
Le soleil fluide et fort

Et sur l'herbe se pavane
La chair rose du printemps

*

Le soir a fermé ses ailes
Sur Paris désespéré
Notre lampe soutient la nuit
Comme un captif la liberté.

III

La source coulant douce et nue
La nuit partout épanouie
La nuit où nous nous unissons
Dans une lutte faible et folle

*

Et la nuit qui nous fait injure
La nuit où se creuse le lit
Vide de la solitude
L'avenir d'une agonie.

IV

C'est une plante qui frappe
A la porte de la terre
Et c'est un enfant qui frappe
A la porte de sa mère
C'est la pluie et le soleil

II

Day of our eye peopled
Better than the greatest battles

Cities and towns and villages
Of our eyes conquerors of time

In the cool valley burns
The strong and liquid sun

And over the grass floats proudly
The pink flesh of springtime

*

Evening has folded its wings
Over Paris in despair
Our lamp holds up the night
As a captive does freedom.

III

The spring flowing sweet and free
The all invading night
The night we join together
In a weak and foolish struggle

*

And the night that does us wrong
The night when the bed grows hollow
Empty of solitude
The future of an agony.

IV

It is a plant that beats
At the earth's door
And it is a child that beats
At its mother's door
It is the rain and the sun

Qui naissent avec l'enfant
Grandissent avec la plante
Fleurissent avec l'enfant

J'entends raisonner et rire

*

On a calculé la peine
Qu'on peut faire à un enfant
Tant de honte sans vomir
Tant de larmes sans périr

Un bruit de pas sous la voûte
Noire et béate d'horreur
On vient déterrer la plante
On vient avilir l'enfant

Par la misère et l'ennui.

V

Le coin du cœur disaient-ils gentiment
Le coin d'amour et de haine et de gloire
Répondions-nous et nos yeux reflétaient
La vérité qui nous servait d'asile

Nous n'avons jamais commencé
Nous nous sommes toujours aimés
Et parce que nous nous aimons
Nous voulons libérer les autres
De leur solitude glacée
Nous voulons et je dis je veux
Je dis tu veux et nous voulons
Que la lumière perpétue
Des couples brillants de vertu
Des couples cuirassés d'audace
Parce que leurs yeux se font face

Et qu'ils ont leur but dans la vie des autres.

Born with the child
Growing with the plant
Flowering with the child

I hear reasoning and laughter

*

The harm has been measured
That can be done to a child
So much shame without sickness
So many tears without death

A sound of footsteps under the vaults
Black and holy in horror
They come to dig up the plant
They come to defile the child

Through misery and weariness.

V

The province of the heart they said sweetly
The province of love and hate and glory
We answered and our eyes reflected
The truth that gave us sanctuary

We never did begin
We always loved each other
And because we love each other
We want to free others
From their icy solitude
We want and I am saying I Want
I am saying You Want and We Want
The light to be everlasting
Couples in the beams of virtue
Couples shielded by their daring
Because their eyes meet

Because their aim is in the lives of others.

VI

Nous ne vous chantons pas trompettes
Pour mieux vous montrer le malheur
Tel qu'il est très grand très bête
Et plus bête d'être entier

Nous prétendions seule la mort
Seule la terre nous limite
Mais maintenant c'est la honte
Qui nous mure tout vivants

Honte du mal illimité
Honte de nos bourreaux absurdes
Toujours les mêmes toujours
Le mêmes amants d'eux-mêmes

Honte des trains de suppliciés
Honte des mots terre brûlée
Mais nous n'avons pas honte de notre souffrance
Mais nous n'avons pas honte d'avoir honte

Derrière les guerriers fuyards
Même plus ne vit un oiseau
L'air est vide de sanglots
Vide de notre innocence

Retentissant de haine et de vengeance.

VII

Au nom du front parfait profond
Au nom des yeux que je regarde
Et de la bouche que j'embrasse
Pour aujourd'hui et pour toujours

Au nom de l'espoir enterré
Au nom des larmes dans le noir
Au nom des plaintes qui font rire
Au nom des rires qui font peur

VI

We do not sing to you with fanfares
Better to lay misfortune bare
Show how huge it is how ugly
And uglier for being absolute

We claimed only death
Only earth restricts
But now it is shame
Enclosing us alive

Shame of boundless evil
Shame of our idiot tormentors
Always the same always
The same ones in love with themselves

Shame of the condemned trains
Shame of the words scorched earth
But we are unashamed of our suffering
But we are unashamed of being ashamed

After the fugitive warriors
Even no bird lives
The air is empty of sobs
Empty of our innocence

Echoing hate and vengeance.

VII

In the name of the deep and perfect brow
In the name of the eyes I behold
And the mouth I kiss
For this day and ever

In the name of buried hope
In the name of tears in darkness
In the name of grievance turned to laughter
In the name of laughter turned to fear

Au nom des rires dans la rue
De la douceur qui lie nos mains
Au nom des fruits couvrant les fleurs
Sur une terre belle et bonne

Au nom des hommes en prison
Au nom des femmes déportées
Au nom de tous nos camarades
Martyrisés et massacrés
Pour n'avoir pas accepté l'ombre

Il nous faut drainer la colère
Et faire se lever le fer
Pour préserver l'image haute
Des innocents partout traqués
Et qui partout vont triompher.

In the name of laughter in the street
Of the gentleness that binds our hands
In the name of fruits that shelter blossoms
Over the rich good earth

In the name of imprisoned men
In the name of deported women
In the name of all our comrades
Martyred and slain
For not accepting darkness

We must drain the wells of anger
Make the sword rise up
To keep alive the shining likeness
Of the guiltless hunted everywhere
Who everywhere shall overcome.

1943

ATHÉNA

Peuple grec peuple roi peuple désespéré
Tu n'as plus rien à perdre que la liberté
Ton amour de la liberté de la justice
Et l'infini respect que tu as de toi-même

Peuple roi tu n'es pas menacé de mourir
Tu es semblable à ton amour tu es candide
Et ton corps et ton cœur ont faim d'éternité
Peuple roi tu as cru que le pain t'était dû

Et que l'on te donnait honnêtement des armes
Pour sauver ton honneur et rétablir ta loi
Peuple désespéré ne te fie qu'à tes armes
On t'en a fait la charité fais-en l'espoir

Oppose cet espoir à la lumière noire
A la mort sans pardon qui n'a plus pied chez toi
Peuple désespéré mais peuple de héros
Peuple de meurt-de-faim gouramands de leur patrie

Petit et grand à la mesure de ton temps
Peuple grec à jamais maître de tes désirs
La chair et l'idéal de la chair conjugués
Les désirs naturels la liberté le pain

La liberté pareille à la mer au soleil
Le pain pareil aux dieux le pain qui joint les hommes
Le bien réel et lumineux plus fort que tout
Plus fort que la douleur et que nos ennemis.

ATHENA

Greek people majestic people desperate people
You have nothing left to lose but freedom
Your love of justice love of liberty
And the endless respect you have for yourselves

Majestic people dying does not threaten you
You are guileless you are like your love
Your heart and body hunger for eternity
Majestic people you believed bread was your due

And that in good faith you were given arms
To save your honour and restore your law
Desperate people trust only in your arms
They were from charity turn them into hope

Set this hope against the shades of darkness
Against the unforgiving death now alien in your home
Desperate people but a people made of heroes
Starvelings yet greedy for their fatherland

Great and humble as your days demanded
Greek people always ruler of desire
Flesh and the flesh's vision joined together
The home-bred longing liberty and bread

This freedom like the sun and like the sea
Bread like the gods this brotherhood of bread
The real and shining wealth stronger than everything
Stronger than sorrow and our enemies.

1944

89

LE MÊME JOUR POUR TOUS

I

L'épée qu'on n'enfonce pas dans le cœur des maîtres des
    coupables
On l'enfonce dans le cœur des pauvres et des innocents

Les premiers yeux sont d'innoncence
Et les seconds de pauvreté
Il faut savoir les protéger

Je ne veux condamner l'amour
Que si je ne tue pas la haine
Et ceux qui me l'ont inspirée

II

Un petit oiseau marche dans d'immenses régions
Où le soleil a des ailes

III

Elle riait autour de moi
Autour de moi elle était nue

Elle était comme une forêt
Comme une foule de femmes
Autour de moi
Comme une armure contre le désert
Comme une armure contre l'injustice

L'injustice frappait partout
Étoile unique étoile inerte d'un ciel gras qui est la privation
    de la lumière

THE SAME DAY FOR ALL

I

The sword that is not thrust into the hearts of lords and the
  guilty
Is thrust into the hearts of the poor and simple

The first eyes are of innocence
And the second of poverty
We must know how to shield them

I want to condemn love
Only if I do not slay hatred
And those who have driven me to hate

II

A small bird steps into vast regions
Where the sun has wings

III

She was laughing around me
Around me she was naked

She was like a forest
Like a multitude of women
Around me
Like armour against the wasteland
Like armour against wrong

Injustice struck high and low
A single star dull star of a rich sky that is the light's
  privation

L'injustice frappait les innocents et les héros les insensés
Qui sauront un jour régner

Car je les entendais rire
Dans leur sang dans leur beauté
Dans la misère et les tortures
Rire d'un rire à venir
Rire à la vie et naître au rire.

Injustice struck at the guiltless and heroes and fools
Who one day will know how to rule

For I heard them laughing
In their beauty in their blood
In misery and torment
Laughing at laughter to come
Laughing at life and being born to laughter.

1944

EN PLEIN MOIS D'AOÛT

En plein mois d'août un lundi soir de couleur tendre
Un lundi soir pendu aux nues
Dans Paris clair comme un œuf frais
En plein mois d'août notre pays aux barricades
Paris osant montrer ses yeux
Paris osant crier victoire
En plein mois d'août un lundi soir

Puisqu'on a compris la lumière
Pourra-t-il faire nuit ce soir
Puisque l'espoir sort des pavés
Sort des fronts et des poings levés
Nous allons imposer l'espoir
Nous allons imposer la vie
Aux esclaves qui désespèrent

En plein mois d'août nous oublions l'hiver
Comme on oublie la politesse des vainqueurs
Leurs grands saluts à la misère et à la mort
Nous oublions l'hiver comme on oublie la honte
En plein mois d'août nous ménageons nos munitions
Avec raison et la raison c'est notre haine
Ô rupture de rien rupture indispensable

La douceur d'être en vie la douleur de savoir
Que nos frères sont morts pour que nous vivions libres
Car vivre et faire vivre est au fond de nous tous
Voici la nuit voici le miroir de nos rêves
Voici minuit minuit point d'honneur de la nuit
La douceur et le deuil de savoir qu'aujourd'hui
Nous avons tous ensemble compromis la nuit.

RIGHT IN THE MIDDLE OF THE MONTH
OF AUGUST

Right in the middle of the month of August a Monday
    evening of soft colours
A Monday evening lost in the clouds
In Paris bright as a fresh egg
Right in the middle of the month of August our country on
    the barricades
Paris daring to show her eyes
Paris daring to shout victory
Right in the middle of the month of August a Monday evening

Since the light has been understood
Will it grow dark this evening
Since hope comes out of paving stones
Comes out of brows and clenched fists
We shall inflict hope
We shall inflict life
On slaves who despair

Right in the middle of the month of August we forget winter
As the politeness of conquerors is forgotten
Their fine salutes to misery and death
We forget winter as shame is forgotten
Right in the middle of the month of August we are sparing
    of munitions
With reason and the reason is our hate
O break from nothing indispensable break

The sweetness of being alive the sorrow of knowing
That our brothers died that we might live free
For to live and help others to live is in the heart of all of us
Here is the night here is the mirror of our dreams
Here is midnight midnight point of honour of the night
The sweetness and the grief of knowing that today
We have all together compromised the night.

1944

GABRIEL PÉRI

Un homme est mort qui n'avait pour défense
Que ses bras ouverts à la vie
Un homme est mort qui n'avait d'autre route
Que celle où l'on hait les fusils
Un homme est mort qui continue la lutte
Contre la mort contre l'oubli

Car tout ce qu'il voulait
Nous le voulions aussi
Nous le voulions aujourd'hui
Que le bonheur soit la lumière
Au fond des yeux au fond du cœur
Et la justice sur la terre

Il y a des mots qui font vivre
Et ce sont des mots innocents
Le mot chaleur le mot confiance
Amour justice et le mot liberté
Le mot enfant et le mot gentillesse
Et certains noms de fleurs et certains noms de fruits
Le mot courage et le mot découvrir
Et le mot frère et le mot camarade
Et certains noms de pays de villages
Et certains noms de femmes et d'amis
Ajoutons-y Péri
Péri est mort pour ce qui nous fait vivre
Tutoyons-le sa poitrine est trouée
Mais grâce à lui nous nous connaissons mieux
Tutoyons-nous son espoir est vivant.

---

* Gabriel Péri (1902-41), politician and journalist, joined the staff of *l'Humanité* in 1934. He became a member of the central committee of the French Communist Party in 1929, deputy for Seine-et-Oise in 1932 and, in 1936, vice-chairman of the Foreign Affairs Commission of the Chamber of Deputies. He wrote illegal

GABRIEL PÉRI*

A man has died who had no other shield
Than his arms open wide to life
A man has died who had no other road
Than the road where rifles are hated
A man has died who battles still
Against death against oblivion

For all the things he wanted
We wanted too
We want them to-day
Happiness to be the light
Within the heart within the eyes
And justice on earth

There are words that help us to live
And they are plain words
The word warmth the word trust
Love justice and the word freedom
The word child and the word kindnesss
The names of certain flowers and certain fruits
The word courage and the word discover
The word brother and the word comrade
The name of certain lands and villages
The names of women and friends
Now let us add the name of Péri
Péri has died for all that gives us life
Let's call him friend his chest is bullet-torn
But thanks to him we know each other better
Let's call each other friend his hope lives on.

1944

Communist literature during the Nazi occupation, was arrested
in May 1941 and shot by the Germans with other hostages on 15
December, 1941.

97

LES ARMES DE LA DOULEUR

à la mémoire de Lucien Legros
fusillé pour ses dix-huit ans.

I

Daddy des Ruines
Homme au chapeau troué
Homme aux orbites creuses
Homme au feu noir
Homme au ciel vide
Corbeau fait pour vivre vieux
Tu avais rêvé d'être heureux

Daddy des Ruines
Ton fils est mort
Assassiné

Daddy la Haine
Ô victime cruelle
Mon camarade des deux guerres
Notre vie est tailladée
Saignante et laide
Mais nous jurons
De tenir bientôt le couteau

Daddy l'Espoir
L'espoir des autres
Tu es partout.

II

J'avais dans mes serments bâti trois châteaux
Un pour la vie un pour la mort un pour l'amour

98

THE ARMS OF SORROW

In memory of Lucien Legros,
shot for his 18th birthday.

to the Father . . .

I

Daddy[1] of the Ruins
Man of the battered hat
Man of the sunken eyes
Man of the dead fire
Man of the empty sky
Old crow made to live old age
You who had dreamed of being happy

Daddy of the Ruins
Your son is dead
Murdered

Daddy Hatred
O cruel victim
My comrade of two wars
Our lives are cut to shreds
Unsightly bleeding
But we vow that soon
We shall be holding the knife

> Daddy Hope
> The hope of others
> You are everywhere.

and the Mother speaks . . .

II

In my pledges I had built three mansions
One for life one for death one for love

Je cachais comme un trésor
Les pauvres petites peines
De ma vie heureuse et bonne

J'avais dans la douceur tissé trois manteaux
Un pour nous deux et deux pour notre enfant
Nous avions les mêmes mains
Et nous pensions l'un pour l'autre
Nous embellissions la terre

J'avais dans la nuit compté trois lumières
Le temps de dormir tout se confondait
Fils d'espoir et fleur miroir œil et lune
Homme sans saveur mais clair de langage
Femme sans éclat mais fluide aux doigts

Brusquement c'est le désert
Et je me perds dans le noir
L'ennemi' s'est révélé
Je suis seule dans ma chair
Je suis seule pour aimer.

III

Cet enfant aurait pu mentir
Et se sauver

La molle plaine infranchissable
Cet enfant n'aimait pas mentir
Il cria très fort ses forfaits

Il opposa sa vérité
La vérité
Comme une épée à ses bourreaux
Comme une épée sa loi suprême

I used to hide like treasure
The paltry little worries
Of my right and happy life

In sweet nature I had spun three coats
One for us two and two for our child
    We had the same hands
    And we always thought alike
    We made earth bloom

In the night I had counted three lights
In my sleep they were the same to me
Son of hope and flower mirror eye and moon
Man of no taste but plain of speaking
Woman of no spark but quick of finger

    Suddenly it is the wilderness
    And I lose my way in the dark
    The enemy is standing there
    I am alone in my body
    I am alone for love.

Her son, this child . . .[2]

III

    This child could have lied
    And gone free

    The impassable lifeless plain
    This child would not tell lies
    He proclaimed aloud his crimes

He set his truth
Truth
Before his tormentors like a sword
His supreme law like a sword

101

Et ses bourreaux se sont vengés
Ils ont fait défiler la mort
L'espoir la mort l'espoir la mort
Ils l'ont gracié puis ils l'ont tué

On l'avait durement traité
Ses pieds ses mains étaient brisés
Dit le gardien du cimetière.

IV

Une seule pensée une seule passion
Et les armes de la douleur

V

Des combattants saignant le feu
Ceux qui feront la paix sur terre
Des ouvriers des paysans
Des guerriers mêlés à la foule
Et quels prodiges de raison
Pour mieux frapper

Des guerriers comme des ruisseaux
Partout sur les champs desséchés
Ou battant d'ailes acharnées
Le ciel boueux pour effacer
La morale de fin du monde
Des oppresseurs

Et selon l'amour la haine

Des guerriers selon l'espoir
Selon le sens de la vie
Et la commune parole
Selon la passion de vaincre
Et de réparer le mal
Qu'on nous a fait

And his tormentors took their revenge
They paraded before him death
Hope death hope death
They pardoned him then slew him

They had cruelly treated him
His feet and hands were crushed
The cemetery keeper said.

IV

A single thought a single passion
And the arms of sorrow.

V

Fighters bleeding fire
They who will make peace on earth
Workers peasants
Warriors mixing with the crowd
And what miracles of reason
The better to strike

Warriors like streams
Running through the parched fields
Or the beating of relentless wings
The clogging sky to wipe away
The rotten values
Of oppressors

And hate in order to love

Warriors in the image of hope
In the image of life's meaning
And the common word
In the image of the passion to conquer
And to right the wrongs
Done to us

Des guerriers selon mon cœur
Celui-ci pense à la mort
Celui-là n'y pense pas
L'un dort l'autre ne dort pas
Mais tous font le même rêve
Se libérer

Chacun est l'ombre de tous.

VI

Les uns sombres les autres nus
Chantant leur bien mâchant leur mal
Mâchant le poids de leur corps
Ou chantant comme on s'envole

Par mille rêves humains
Par mille voies de nature
Ils sortent de leur pays
Et leur pays entre en eux
De l'air passe dans leur sang

Leur pays peut devenir
Le vrai pays des merveilles
Le pays de l'innocence.

VII

Des réfractaires selon l'homme
Sous le ciel de tous les hommes
Sur la terre unie et pleine

Au-dedans de ce fruit mûr
Le soleil comme un cœur pur
Tout le soleil pour les hommes

Tous les hommes pour les hommes
La terre entière et le temps
Le bonheur dans un seul corps.

Warriors in the image of my heart
This one thinks of death
That one does not
One sleeps the other wakes
But all dream the same dream
To be free

Each is the shadow of all.

VI

Some gloomy others plain
Singing of blessings cursing misfortunes
Cursing the burden of their bodies
Or singing as one takes to flight

Through a thousand human dreams
Through a thousand natural ways
They leave their native land
And their native land returns to them
Air seeps into their blood

Their land can become
The true land of wonder
The land of innocence.

VII

Rebels in the image of man
Under the skies of all men
On the replete united earth

Within the ripe fruit
The sun like a pure heart
The whole sun for men

Every man for men
The whole earth and time
Happiness in a single body.

*

Je dis ce que je vois
Ce que je sais
Ce qui est vrai.

*

I tell of what I see
What I know
What is true.

1944

1. The English word is used by Eluard in the original French text.

2. Lucien Legros, a student of seventeen, was arrested after a school demonstration in April 1942 and sentenced to forced labour by a Vichy French court. He was then handed over to the Gestapo and shot as a hostage after numerous promises of freedom and threats of execution.

EN AVRIL 1944:
PARIS RESPIRAIT ENCORE!

Nous descendions vers le fleuve fidèle: ni son flot, ni nos yeux n'abandonnaient Paris.

Non pas ville petite, mais enfantine et maternelle.

*

Ville au travers de tout comme un sentier d'été, plein de fleurs et d'oiseaux comme un baiser profond plein d'enfants souriants, plein de mères fragiles.

*

Non pas ville ruinée, mais ville compliquée, marquée par sa nudité.

*

Ville entre nos poignets comme un lien rompu, entre nos yeux comme un œil déjà vu, ville répétée comme un poème.

Ville ressemblante.

*

Vieille ville . . . Entre la ville et l'homme, il n'y avait même plus l'épaisseur d'un mur.

Ville de la transparence, ville innocente.

*

Il n'y avait plus, entre l'homme seul et la ville déserte, que l'épaisseur d'un miroir.

Il n'y avait plus qu'une ville aux couleurs de l'homme, terre et chair, sang et sève.

*

IN APRIL 1944: PARIS
WAS STILL BREATHING!

We came down to the faithful river: neither its flood nor our
eyes forsook Paris.

Not a mean city, but a city childlike and motherly.

*

A city like a winding path in summer, filled with flowers and
birds, like a long kiss filled with smiling children, filled
with delicate mothers.

Not a city despoiled, but a bewildering city, bearing her
nakedness.

*

A city between our hands like a broken bond, between our
eyes like an eye already seen, a city sung again like a
poem.

A city built in our own image.

*

An old city . . . Between the city and man there remained
not even the thickness of a wall.

*

A city of transparence, a guiltless city.

*

Between man alone and the deserted city there was nothing
but the thickness of a mirror.

Nothing but a city in the colours of man, earth and flesh,
blood and strength.

*

Le jour qui joue dans l'eau la nuit qui meurt sur terre
Le rhythme de l'air pur est plus fort que la guerre.

Ville à la main tendue et tout le monde de rire et tout le
monde de jouir, ville exemplaire.

*

Nul ne put briser les ponts qui nous menaient au sommeil
et du sommeil à nos rêves et de nos rêves à l'éternité.

Ville durable où j'ai vécu notre victoire sur la mort.

The day that plays in the water, the night that dies on earth. The rhythm of pure air is stronger than war.

A city with an outstretched hand, and then comes all the laughing world and all the revelling world, a city to behold.

*

No one could hurl down the bridges that led us to sleep and from sleep to our dreams and from our dreams to eternity.

An enduring city where I have lived through our victory over death.

1945

SAINT-ALBAN

L'eau dans les prés de la montagne
Continue à nos pieds de chanter,mollement
Il fait frais le soir tombe et nous réunissons
Nos yeux sur le chemin que nous savons par cœur

Nos jeunes amis nous attendent
It fait bon vivre à la campagne
Nos feuilles vont regagner l'arbre
Notre herbe retrouver la nuit de sa croissance

Ce soir il y aura des rires quelques larmes
S'y mêleront l'amour baptisera la nuit
De noms nouveaux à la couleur de nos corps nus
Rose mettra son bonnet rouge

Blanche perdra son bonnet noir.

AT SAINT-ALBAN

The water in the mountain meadows
Flows past our feet like a lazy song
The air is cool and evening comes we join
Our eyes upon the road we know by heart

Our young friends expect us
It is good to live in the country
Our leaves will find the tree again
Our grass the night of its increase

This night there will be laughter a few tears
Will mingle there and love will bless the night
With new names coloured in our nakedness
Rose will wear her red bonnet

Blanche will lose her black bonnet.

1945

LE BAISER

Toute tiède encore du linge annulé
Tu fermes les yeux et tu bouges
Comme bouge un chant qui naît
Vaguement mais de partout

Odorante et savoureuse
Tu dépasses sans te perdre
Les frontières de ton corps

Tu as enjambé le temps
Te voici femme nouvelle
Révélée à l'infini.

THE KISS

Still warm from sleep gown cast away
You drift but you have closed your eyes
Drift like a new song comes to life
Faintly yet from everywhere

Sweet delectable you float
Past your body's boundaries
And you do not lose your way

You have stridden over time
New-born woman you are here
For infinity to see.

1945

COMME BEAUCOUP D'AUTRES

De guerre en guerre je vieillis
J'aurai un jour de beaux souvenirs
Souvenirs de pieds dans la boue
De visages à faire peur
De contraintes à rendre idiot
De tortures à faire trahir
Souvenirs de villes brisées
De ruines molles et rampantes
Arrosées de feu et de sang
J'aurai connu des terroristes
Des communistes et des Juifs
J'aurai connu l'espoir stérile
Et des misères ridicules
J'aurai connu la liberté d'être soumis
La faveur de mourir de faim
Et la faveur de mourir vite
Des enfants bons à tuer
Pour achever les guerres
Et des hommes bafoués
Pour couronner la paix

J'aurai quand même de beaux souvenirs
J'aurai connu toutes les hontes
Mais aussi toutes les fiertés
J'aurai connu l'espoir des justes
Leur passion d'une vie meilleure
J'aurai connu des innocents
Des communistes des complices
Contre la mort contre la haine
Et des petits enfants riant
A l'aurore toujours nouvelle

J'aurai quand même de beaux souvenirs
Mariés à ma vieillesse verte.

LIKE MANY OTHERS

From one war to another I grew old
One day I shall have happy memories
Memories of feet held in the mud
Faces to make you feel afraid
Rules to make a fool of you
Hell to make you cry aloud
Memories of broken towns
Ruins and the nameless waste
Blessed with holy blood and fire
I shall have known the partisans
Communists and Jews
I shall have known the emptiness of hope
And mocking miseries
I shall have known what free submission was
The favour of starvation all the grace
And privilege of dying fast as well
Children good enough for killing
To finish off the wars
And men left scorned and spurned
Just to crown the peace.

I shall have happy memories just the same
I shall have known the sum of infamy
And all the pride as well
I shall have known the hopes of righteous men
Their passion for a better life
I shall have known the simple artless folk
Communists and friends
All enemies of death and hate
And the little children laughing
At every break of day.

I shall have happy memories just the same
Blended with my green old age.

1946

À LA MÉMOIRE
DE PAUL VAILLANT-COUTURIER

J'habite le Quartier de la Chapelle
Et le journal de ma cellule s'intitule
Les Amis de la Rue vous parlent
On ne le vend pas on le distribue
Il ne nous coûte rien qu'un peu de notre temps

Et mon cœur est avec les Amis de la Rue
Ils me parlent ils m'encouragent
A être un homme de la rue
Multiplié par l'amitié par le désir
D'être ensemble pour être forts

Dans ma rue les passants ont les mêmes soucis
Et les mêmes espoirs d'un peu moins de malheur
Mêmes amours aussi mon cœur est avec eux
Mon cœur est tout entier dans leur cœur innocent
Je le sais je parle pour eux

Ils parlent pour moi nos mots sont les mêmes
Notre rue mène à d'autres rues à d'autres hommes
A d'autres temps et dans le temps à toi

IN MEMORY
OF PAUL VAILLANT-COUTURIER*

I live in La Chapelle district
and the news-sheet of my Party cell is called
Friends in the Street
It is not for sale
it is given away
it costs us nothing
except a little free time

And my heart is with Friends in the Street
they talk to me
encourage me
to be someone in the street
made many by friendship
by the wish
to be together in order to be strong

In my street passers-by
have the same cares
the same hopes
of a little less misfortune
the same loves too
my heart is with them
all my heart is in their innocent hearts
I know
I speak for them

They speak for me
we speak the same language
one street leads to other streets
to other people
to other days
and in your own day

Paul Vaillant-Couturier qui fus semblable à nous
Et qui jurais par nous et nous jurons par toi

Qu'un jour la vie sera meilleure.

Paul Vaillant-Couturier
you were one of us
and swore by us
as we swear by you

that life will be better one day.

1946

---

* A founder member of the French Communist Party and former editor-in-chief of *l'Humanité*.

EN ESPAGNE

S'il y a en Espagne un arbre teint de sang
C'est l'arbre de la liberté

S'il y a en Espagne une bouche bavarde
Elle parle de liberté

S'il y a en Espagne un verre de vin pur
C'est le peuple qui le boira.

IN SPAIN

If in Spain there is one bloodstained tree
It is the tree of freedom

If in Spain there is one chattering mouth
It speaks of freedom

If in Spain there is one glass of pure wine
It is the people who will drink it.

1948

DIALOGUE

Belle invention est couverte de honte
Mémoire d'or est enrobée de plomb
Amour glorieux est jeté hors du lit
Noble nature est souillée par des nains

Venez voir le sang dans les rues

Sommes plusieurs à refuser
Que le soleil soit un couteau
Et que la mer soit un poison
Sommes nombreux à vouloir vivre

Rien ni même la victoire
Ne comblera le vide terrible du sang:
Rien, ni la mer, ni les pas
Du sable et du temps
Ni le géranium brûlant
Sur la sépulture.

Trop d'entre nous ont quitté vie
Par espoir d'un monde meilleur
Trop d'innocents sûrs de leur droit
Je leur souris ils me sourient

Un visage aux yeux morts surveille les ténèbres
Son épée est gonflée d'espérances terrestres

Gravité de sens et de sexe
Vaisseau de matière subtile
Nous sommes sur un seul rameau
Feuilles et fruits pour servir l'arbre

DIALOGUE

Fine invention is covered in shame
Golden memory is clothed in lead
Glorious love is thrown from the couch
Noble nature is sullied by dwarfs

Come and see the blood in the streets

A lot of us deny
That the sun is a knife
That the sea is poison
A lot of us want to live

Nothing, not even victory
Will fill the terrible emptiness of blood:
Nothing, neither sea nor traces
In sand and time
Nor the burning geranium
On the burial ground.

Too many of us have died
Hoping for a better world
Too many guiltless certain of their rights
I smile at them they smile at me

A face with dead eyes watches over the darkness,
Its sword is swollen with earthly hopes.

Depth of meaning and sex
Fabric of beguiling substance
We are on a single bough
Leaves and fruit to serve the tree

Seul exercice la bonté
Seule manœuvre la raison
Avec ses mille et mille oiseaux
Portés de planète en planète

Fils préférés de la victoire, tant de fois tombés,
Aux mains tant de fois effacées

Toujours le mot victoire ô mon cœur j'ai confiance
Image des images le matin s'ajourne
Mais il est là déjà puisque nous en parlons
Rêve soleil nocturne a le poids de toujours

O! mères traversées par l'angoisse et la mort,
Regardez le cœur du noble jour qui naît
Et sachez que vos morts sourient de cette terre
Et que leurs poings levés tremblent au-dessus du blé

Je veux faire fleurir la rondeur cramoisie
Du ciel sur terre et de la possession
Haine n'est rien amour s'inscrit au double
Quand l'un faiblit les deux se décolorent

J'ai vu avec ces yeux que j'ai, avec ce cœur qui regarde,
J'ai vu arriver les combattants clairs, les combattants dominateurs
De la svelte, de la dure, de la mûre, de l'ardente brigade de
    pierre.

Que le plus clair courage éclaire le langage
Homme traqué devient la perfection future.

Only duty goodness
Only contrivance reason
With its thousand birds
Borne from planet to planet

Favourite sons of victory, so many times fallen,
Their hands so many times worn away.

The word victory for ever O heart I have trust
Image of images the morning defers
But morning is here since we speak of it
Dreams and sun the night's eternal burden

O mothers run through by death and anguish
Watch the heart of the noble day bursting;
Know that your dead smile from this land,
That their raised fists shake above the corn.

I want to make bloom on earth
The crimson sweep of sky and of possession
Hate is nothing love signs for both
When one gives way both fade

I have seen with these eyes I have, with this beholding heart,
I have seen come the shining warriors, the arrogant,
The lithe and harsh and ragged ones, from out the ardent ranks of
*   stone.*

Let the brightest courage light up speech
The hunted man shall be the future faultlessness.

1948

The lines in italics are taken from poems by Pablo Neruda.

LE MONT GRAMMOS

Le mont Grammos est un peu rude
Mais les hommes l'adoucissent

Les barbares nous les tuons
Nous abrégeons notre nuit

Plus bêtes que poudre à canon
Nos ennemis nous ignorent

Ils ne savent rien de l'homme
Ni de son pouvoir insigne

Notre cœur polit la pierre.

MOUNT GRAMMOS

Mount Grammos is harsh enough
But men tame it

Barbarians we slay
Our night we make brief

Duller than gunpowder
Our enemies do not know us

They know nothing of men
Nor of their uncommon powers

Our hearts polish the stone.

1949

PRIÈRE
DES VEUVES ET DES MÈRES

Nous avions accordé nos mains
Et nos yeux riaient sans raison

Par les armes et par le sang
Délivrez-nous du fascisme

Nous bercions toute la lumière
Et nos seins se gonflaient de lait

Laissez-nous tenir un fusil
Pour tirer sur les fascistes

Nous étions la source et le fleuve
Nous rêvions d'être l'océan

Donnez-nous juste le moyen
De ne pas gracier les fascistes

Ils sont moins nombreux que nos morts
Nos morts n'avaient tué personne

Nous nous aimions sans y penser
Sans rien comprendre que la vie

Laissez-nous tenir un fusil
Et nous mourrons contre la mort.

PRAYER
OF WIDOWS AND MOTHERS

We had given our hands
And our eyes laughed for no reason

By arms and blood
Deliver us from fascism

We rocked cradles the day long
And our breasts were swollen with milk

Let us hold a rifle
To shoot at fascists

We were the source and the river
We dreamed of being the ocean

Give us only the means
Not to forgive fascists

They are fewer than our dead
Our dead had killed no one

We loved one another without thinking
Understanding nothing but life

Let us hold a rifle
And we shall die against death.

1949

POUR NE PLUS ÊTRE SEULS

Comme un flot d'oiseaux noirs ils dansaient dans la nuit
Et leur cœur était pur on ne voyait plus bien
Quels étaient les garçons quelles étaient les filles

Tous avaient leur fusil au dos

Se tenant par la main ils dansaient ils chantaient
Un air ancien nouveau un air de liberté
L'ombre en était illuminée elle flambait

L'ennemi s'était endormi

Et l'écho répétait leur amour de la vie
Et leur jeunesse était comme une plage immense
Où la mer vient offrir tous les baisers du monde

Peu d'entre eux avaient vu la mer

Pourtant bien vivre est un voyage sans frontières
Ils vivaient bien vivant entre eux et pour leurs frères
Leurs frères de partout ils en rêvaient tout haut

Et la montagne allait vers la plaine et la plage
Reproduisant leur rêve et leur folle conquête
La main allant aux mains comme source à la mer.

NO MORE ALONE

Like a flight of black birds they danced into the night
And their hearts were pure you could no longer tell
Who were the boys who were the girls

They all had rifles on their backs

Holding hands they danced they sang
An old song a new song then a song of freedom
It lit the darkness and the darkness blazed

The enemy had fallen asleep

And the echo told again of their love of life
And their youth was like a vast shore
Where the sea came to offer all the kisses of the world

Few of them had seen the sea

Yet to live with honour is a journey without frontiers
They lived with honour for one another and for their
    comrades
Their comrades from everywhere they dreamed of them
    aloud

And the mountain went down to the plain and the
    sands
Recalling their dreams and their wild conquests
A hand that reaches for hands as a spring reaches for the
    sea.

1949

LE VISAGE DE LA PAIX

1

Je connais tous les lieux où la colombe loge
Et le plus naturel est la tête de l'homme.

2

L'amour de la justice et de la liberté
A produit un fruit merveilleux
Un fruit qui ne se gâte point
Car il a le goût du bonheur.

3

Que la terre produise que la terre fleurisse
Que la chair et le sang vivants
Ne soient jamais sacrifiés.

4

Que le visage humain connaisse
L'utilité de la beauté
Sous l'aile de la réflexion.

5

Pour tous du pain pour tous des roses
Nous avons tous prêté serment
Nous marchons à pas de géant
Et la route n'est pas si longue.

6

Nous fuirons le repos nous fuirons le sommeil
Nous prendrons de vitessse l'aube et le printemps
Et nous préparerons des jours et des saisons
A la mesure de nos rêves.

THE FACE OF PEACE

1

I know all the places where the dove dwells
Its most natural home is in the mind of man.

2

The love of justice and freedom
Has borne a wondrous fruit
A fruit that never spoils
For it tastes of gladness.

3

Let the earth produce let the earth bloom
That living flesh and blood
Never be sacrificed.

4

Let human eyes see
The service of beauty
In the shelter of thought.

5

Bread for all roses for all
So have we all sworn
We march with the stride of giants
And the road is not so long.

6

We shall shun rest we shall shun sleep
We shall seize the dawn and spring
And we shall make ready days and seasons
Measured to our dreams.

7

La blanche illumination
De croire tout le bien possible.

8

L'homme en proie à la paix se couronne d'espoir,

9

L'homme en proie à la paix a toujours un sourire
Après tous les combats pour qui le lui demande.

10

Feu fertile des grains des mains et des paroles
Un feu de joie s'allume et chaque cœur a chaud.

11

Vaincre s'appuie sur la fraternité.

12

Grandir est sans limites.

13

Chacun sera vainqueur.

14

La sagesse pend au plafond
Et son regard tombe du front comme une lampe de
  cristal.

15

La lumière descend lentement sur la terre
Du front le plus ancien elle passe au sourire
Des enfants délivrés de la crainte des chaînes.

7

The white vision
Of believing all possible good

8

Man beset by peace wears the crown of hope.

9

Man beset by peace when struggle is done
Has always a smile for the one who seeks it.

10

Abundant fire of seed and hands and speech
A fire of joy lights up and every heart is warm.

11

To conquer is to trust in brotherhood.

12

To grow tall is to know no bounds.

13

Everyone shall be a conqueror.

14

Wisdom is born of our wit
And its gaze falls from the brow like a crystal lamp.

15

The light descends slowly over the earth
From the oldest brow it passes to the smile
Of children freed from fear of chains.

16

Dire qui si longtemps l'homme a fait peur à l'homme
Et fait peur aux oiseaux qu'il portait dans sa tête.

17

Après avoir lavé son visage au soleil
L'homme a besoin de vivre
Besoin de faire vivre et il s'unit d'amour
S'unit à l'avenir.

18

Mon bonheur c'est notre bonheur
Mon soleil c'est notre soleil
Nous nous partageons la vie
L'espace et le temps sont à tous.

19

L'amour est au travail il est infatigable.

20

C'était en mil neuf cent dix sept
Et nous gardons l'intelligence
De notre délivrance.

21

Nous avons inventé autrui
Comme autrui nous a inventé
Nous avions besoin l'un de l'autre.

22

Comme un oiseau volant a confiance en ses ailes
Nous savons où nous mène notre main tendue
Vers notre frère.

16

To say that for so long man has made man fear
And made fear the birds he bore within his head.

17

His face bathed in the sun
Man has need to live
Need to let live and join with love
Join with the future.

18

My happiness is our happiness
My sun is our sun
We share life with each other
Space and time belong to all.

19

Love labours it is tireless.

20

It was the year 1917
And we remember the meaning
Of our deliverance.

21

We discovered others
As others discovered us
We had need of one another.

22

As a bird in flight trusts its wings
We know where leads our hand outstretched
To our brothers.

23

Nous allons combler l'innocence
De la force qui si longtemps
Nous a manqué
Nous ne serons jamais plus seuls.

24

Nos chansons appellent la paix
Et nos réponses sont des actes pour la paix.

25

Ce n'est pas le naufrage c'est notre désir
Qui est fatal et c'est la paix qui est inévitable.

26

L'architecture de la paix
Repose sur le monde entier.

27

Ouvre tes ailes beau visage
Impose au monde d'être sage
Puisque nous devenons réels.

28

Nous devenons réels ensemble par l'effort
Par notre volonté de dissoudre les ombres
Dans le cours fulgurant d'une clarté nouvelle.

29

La force deviendra de plus en plus légère
Nous respirerons mieux nous chanterons plus haut.

We shall feed innocence
With the strength we lacked
For so long
We shall never more be alone.

24

Our songs call for peace
And our answers are acts for peace.

25

It is not disaster but our desire
Which is fatal and it is peace which is inevitable.

26

The mansions of peace
Rest upon the whole world.

27

Open your wings fair face
Impose your wisdom on the world
For we are growing real.

28

We are growing real by deeds together
By our will to scatter the shades
In the flashing flight of a new splendour.

29

Strength will grow lighter and lighter
We shall breathe freer and we shall sing louder.

1951

MARINE

Je te regarde et le soleil grandit
Il va bientôt couvrir notre journée
Éveille-toi cœur et couleur en tête
Pour dissiper les malheurs de la nuit

Je te regarde tout est nu
Dehors les barques ont peu d'eau
Il faut tout dire en peu de mots
La mer est froide sans amour

C'est le commencement du monde
Les vagues vont bercer le ciel
Toi tu te berces dans tes draps
Tu tires le sommeil à toi

Éveille-toi que je suive tes traces
J'ai un corps pour t'attendre pour te suivre
Des portes de l'aube aux portes de l'ombre
Un corps pour passer ma vie à t'aimer

Un cœur pour rêver hors de ton sommeil.

MARINE

I gaze upon you and the sun grows large
Soon it will overwhelm our day
Awake with heart and colour in your head
To chase away the night's bad dreams

I gaze upon you nothing is concealed
Outside the sea-boats lie in shallow water
For everything few words must be enough
The sea is cold without its love

This is the way the world begins
The waves will lull the sky asleep
And you will float in dreams and gather in
The sleep that waits about your bed

Awake that I may follow where you go
I have a body that waits to follow you
From the gates of day to the gates of dusk
A body to spend with you a life of love

A heart to dream beyond your sleep.

1951

143

BONNE JUSTICE

C'est la chaude loi des hommes
Du raisin ils font du vin
Du charbon ils font du feu
Des baisers ils font des hommes

C'est la dure loi des hommes
Se garder intact malgré
Les guerres et la misère
Malgré les dangers de mort

C'est la douce loi des hommes
De changer l'eau en lumière
Le rêve en réalité
Et les ennemis en frères

Une loi vieille et nouvelle
Qui va se perfectionnant
Du fond du cœur de l'enfant
Jusqu'à à la raison suprême.

SOUND JUSTICE

It is the warm law of men
From grapes they make wine
From coal they make fire
From kisses they make men

It is the harsh law of men
To stay alive in spite
Of wars and misery
In spite of death's dangers

It is the gentle law of men
To change water into light
Dreams into reality
Enemies into brothers

A law old and new
Self-perfecting always
From the depth of a child's heart
To supreme reason.

1951

LE PHÉNIX

Je suis le dernier sur ta route
Le dernier printemps la dernière neige
Le dernier combat pour ne pas mourir

Et nous voici plus bas et plus haut que jamais

*

Il y a de tout dans notre bûcher
Des pommes de pin des sarments
Mais aussi des fleurs plus fortes que l'eau

De la boue et de la rosée.

*

La flamme est sous nos pieds la flamme nous couronne
A nos pieds des insectes des oiseaux des hommes
Vont s'envoler

Ceux qui volent vont se poser.

*

Le ciel est clair la terre est sombre
Mais la fumée s'en va au ciel
Le ciel a perdu tous ses feux

La flamme est restée sur la terre.

*

La flamme est la nuée du cœur
Et toutes les branches du sang
Elle chante notre air

Elle dissipe la buée de notre hiver.

*

THE PHOENIX

I am the last on your road
The last spring the last snow
The last fight for living's sake

And we are here lower and higher than ever.

*

All things are in our funeral pyre
Fir cones and shoots of vine
But also flowers stronger than water

And mud and dew.

*

The flame is beneath our feet the flame crowns us
At our feet insects birds and men
Will vanish

Those who fly away will settle.

*

The sky is clear the earth is dark
But smoke rises to the sky
The sky has lost all its fires

The flame has stayed on earth.

*

The flame is the heart's surge
And all the alleys of the blood
It sings of our open air

It scatters our winter's mist.

*

Nocturne et en horreur a flambé le chagrin
Les cendres ont fleuri en joie et en beauté
Nous tournons toujours le dos au couchant

Tout a la couleur de l'aurore.

A night-bird in horror has fired the grief
Ashes have flowered in joy and beauty
We always turn away from the setting sun

All things have the colour of daybreak.

1951

HADJI DIMITRE

Lá-bas, dans le Balkan, il est toujours vivant.
Mais il gît et gémit, il est couvert de sang;
Sa poitrine est trouée d'une affreuse blessure.
Frappé dans sa jeunesse, il vit, notre héros.

Il a laissé tomber son fusil inutile,
Son sabre s'est brisé dans l'ardeur du combat.
Et sa tête vacille et ses yeux s'obscurcissent
Et sa bouche maudit l'univers tout entier.

Il gît, notre héros, tandis qu'en haut du ciel
Le soleil, arrêté, flamboie et se courrouce.
Dans la plaine, très loin, chantent des moissonneuses.
Et le sang se répand, le sang coule sans cesse.

C'est l'époque de la moisson . . . Chantez, esclaves,
Plus tristement! Et toi, soleil, brûle plus fort
Sur la terre asservie! Le héros va mourir,
Il va aussi mourir . . . Mais tais-toi, ô mon cœur,

Car celui qui succombe pour la liberté
Ne meurt pas, ne peut pas mourir! Que sur lui pleurent
La terre et le soleil et toute la nature!
Que les poètes le célèbrent dans leurs chants!

Le jour, l'aigle l'abrite à l'ombre de ses ailes
Et le loup vient lécher tout doucement ses plaies.
Et le faucon, l'oiseau des héros foudroyants,
Veille jalousement sur le héros, son frère.

Voici que le soir tombe et qu'apparaît la lune.
Le ciel va se remplir d'étoiles, goutte à goutte.
La forêt bruit, le vent imperceptible souffle.
Tout le Balkan chante le chant des haïdouks.

150

HADJI DIMITRE[1]

High in the Balkans, he will never die.
But he lies groaning, washed in his own blood;
His breast is shattered by a mortal wound.
Struck down in years of youth, he lives, our hero.

His useless rifle he has thrown aside,
His sword has broken in the battle's rage.
His head is swaying and his eyes grow dim
And from his lips come curses on the world.

Our hero lies, while high in skies above
The sun is still, provoked to anger's fire.
In plains afar, the reaping women sing,
And blood is shed and flows on endlessly.

This is the harvest time . . . Sing sadder, slaves!
And you, O sun, burn brighter in the sky
Upon this captive earth! For heroes die,
He too will die . . . But be at peace, my heart,

For he who perishes in freedom's name
Dies not and cannot die! May on him weep
The earth and sun and nature's wondrous things!
May poets celebrate his deeds in song!

By day the eagle folds him in great wings;
And true in love the wolf comes lick his wounds.
The falcon, bird of ardent warriors,
Watches with jealous eye his hero brother.

Now darkness falls and now the moon appears.
Stars fill the sky like tiny crystal drops.
The forest whispers in the slightest breeze.
The Balkans sing the songs of partisans.

L'heure sonne où les nymphes en parures blanches
Viennent gracieusement se livrer à la danse,
D'un pied léger frôlant à peine l'herbe verte,
Puis auprès du héros se posent, attentives.

De simples des prairies, l'une panse ses plaies,
L'autre humecte ses mains et ses tempes d'eau fraîche.
Et celle qu'il regarde, c'est la plus rieuse,
Sur la bouche lui donne un baiser fugitif.

Dis-mois, ma sœur, où est mon second, Karadja?
Où sont les miens, où est ma droujina fidèle?
Où sont-ils? Réponds-moi, puis emporte mon âme,
C'est ici que je dois et que je veux mourir.

Elles frappent des mains, s'enlacent et s'envolent
Dans la nuit transparente où leurs chansons résonnent;
Elles cherchent aux cieux, jusqu'au lever du jour
    L'âme de Karadja.

L'aurore est apparue! Là-haut, dans la montagne,
Le héros gît, son sang coule, coule toujours.
Le loup lèche à nouveau sa blessure brûlante
    Et le soleil flamboie!

---

1. Hadji Dimitre fell on the heights of Stara Planina in August 1868. He and his followers were surrounded and massacred by a Turkish force twenty times stronger in numbers. The Bulgarian people never believed in his death and legend has it that the hero lives on to fight his battles with the same courage and daring.

2. Christo Botev (1848-1876) was a Bulgarian writer, patriot and an ardent socialist who lived for many years as a refugee in Romania where he played a leading part through his writing in the Bulgarian central revolutionary commitee in Bucarest. He is

The hour strikes when nymphs adorned in white
Come gracefully to enter in the dance;
They gather round the hero, heedfully,
And little light feet stir the cool green grasss.

With sweet herbs of the fields, one binds his wounds,
One bathes his hands and temples from the spring;
And she, the laughing girl he looks upon,
Places a stolen kiss upon his mouth.

'Tell, sister, lives my faithful Karadja?
Where are my followers, my faithful band?
Where are they? Speak, and carry off my soul,
Here I must die and here I wish to die.'

They clap their hands, fold arms, and fly away
To echoing song and night's transparency.
They seek in Heaven's air till break of day
        The soul of Karadja.

The light of dawn! High on the mountain top
The hero lies, his blood is flowing still.
The wolf licks yet again his burning wound
        And the sun flares!

Christo Botev[2]

1952

---

especially renowned for his poetry which expresses his patriotic
and revolutionary ideals, his anti-clericalism, his hatred of
tyranny and his faith in a better future. His poem 'Hadji Dimitre',
adapted into French by Paul Eluard, is considered to be among
the masterpieces of Bulgarian literature. Botev died fighting the
Turkish invaders two years before the liberation of his country.

SIMPLES IMAGES DE DEMAIN

Un homme plus un homme un peuple plus un peuple
Et c'est l'humanité

Un homme et une femme et leur enfant entre eux
L'amour se perpétue

Sur l'heure de midi notre ombre se réduit
Socle d'une statue

Sur l'heure de midi le soleil noue la terre
Et l'on oublie la nuit

Du plus profond de l'herbe au gouffre du ciel clair
Chacun suit son chemin

Et le jour fait merveille entre des mains nouvelles
Dans l'avenir sans fin

L'homme aime son travail son travail et les siens
Par-delà les frontières

Par-delà le passé la femme fait le geste
D'allaiter son enfant

Et l'enfant recommence à penser désirer
Par le commencement

*

Toi d'aujourd'hui que j'aime par-delà moi-même
Comme la vie faite espérance

SIMPLE PICTURES OF TOMORROW

A man and another man a people and another people
That is humanity

A man and a woman and their child between them
Love enduring

At the hour of midday our shadow lessens
A statue's plinth

At the hour of midday the sun binds the earth
And night is forgotten

From the deeps of the grass to the space of the clear sky
Each follows his own road

And the day in new hands shows its wonders
In the endless future

Man loves his work his work and his own kind
Beyond frontiers

Beyond times past woman makes the gestures
Of feeding her child

And the child begins again to think to wish
From the beginning

*

You of this day whom I love beyond myself
Like life made hope

Tu multiples mon cœur et mon corps et mes sens
Et la raison suprême

De croire que le temps n'efface pas la vie
Mais qu'il est la vie même.

You make great my heart my body and my senses
And the supreme reason

For not believing time surpasses life
For time is life itself.

1953